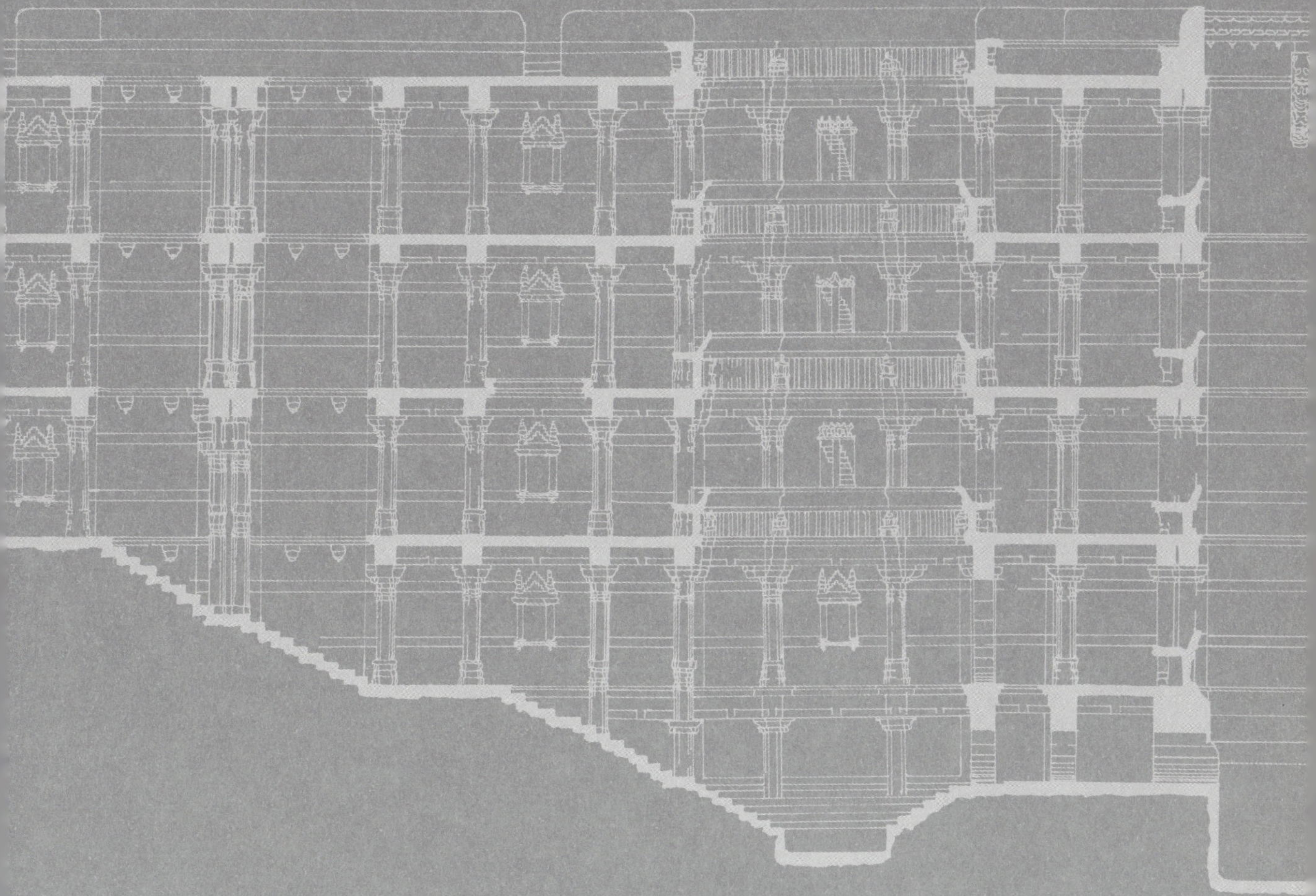

Metonymy in Contemporary Art: A New Paradigm. Denise Green

‘I have known the artist Denise Green for many years and we have had many interesting discussions about her work and her views on art in general. This book, however, came as a surprise, not least because of her colossal reach and her intrepid over-stepping of lines.

I suspect that it is only as an artist that she can make these bold essays into such sensitive and contested areas because, whatever her reasoning, in the end it is her subjective world as an artist that is the stage on which these different cultural discourses can be brought together.

The academic and curatorial world in which I move has been wrestling with the loss of a unifying language of the avant-garde in the context of an inclusive global agenda since 1989. Jean-Hubert Martin put the question to us in *Magiciens de la Terre,* but we have advanced very little in trying to find an incisive critical language to cope with diversity. It may be that the idea of such a discourse is itself antiquated, but for many of us the danger of relativism must be resisted by some coherent system or overlapping systems.

An even greater oversight has been our failure to investigate the subjective and creative implications of all this for artists. Maybe in Green’s book we can begin to see some light at least from within the creative process itself? It is my belief that affect is going to be central to a new way of looking at common ground in art and in politics and this is likely to be found in art before it is adequately described by theory.’

Anthony Bond, Art Gallery of New South Wales, Sydney

‘In this uber-narrative, veering between autobiography and art criticism, artist Denise Green juggles art, life and aesthetic paradigms like a ‘jazz freedom fighter’ in a marathon conversation with the intangibles of her own creativity. Resisting all party lines and drawing on a wide range of sources, she constructs her own model of multicultural influence, blurring and smudging as many boundaries as she can along the way. Readers can be grateful to Green for her example of integrated thinking. It helps to free us all from the isolation of a single Western paradigm which creates unnecessary walls and limits in the mind.’

Suzi Gablik, USA

‘Art is a lifelong learning of new wisdoms and this book brings you back to the origin of art. In *Metonymy in Contemporary Art: A New Paradigm,* Green argues from her current understanding of Indian and Aboriginal aesthetic viewpoints. Walter Benjamin, Clement Greenberg, all the heroes who still dominate art theory, are importantly criticized. However, if you want to learn about A.K. Ramanujan and metonymic thinking, about Aboriginal art, about mythic consciousness, about why the struggle of the life of an artist is to become himself, about artists, such as Agnes Martin, Joseph Beuys and Brice Marden, Alex Katz, Frank Stella, Barry Le Va and Dorothea Rockburne and others, you have to study this book. You will learn that contemporary art can be interpreted from a more global and pluralistic perspective.’

Dieter Ronte, Kunstmuseum, Bonn

Published in the United States by the University of Minnesota Press
111 Third Avenue South, Suite 290
Minneapolis, MN 55401-2520
http://www.upress.umn.edu

Library of Congress Cataloging-in-Publication Data
A Catalog record for this book is available from the Library of Congress

ISBN 0-8166-4878-6 (hc)

The University of Minnesota Press is an equal-opportunity educator and employer.

Published and distributed in Australia by Macmillan Art Publishing,
a division of Palgrave Macmillan • Macmillan Publishers Australia
627 Chapel Street, South Yarra, Victoria 3141, Australia
Telephone: 03 9825 1099 • Facsimile: 03 9825 1010

Designed by Brian Sadgrove

Edited by Jenny Zimmer • Typography by Charles Teuma
Produced by Australian Book Connection, Melbourne, Australia • 2005

Contents

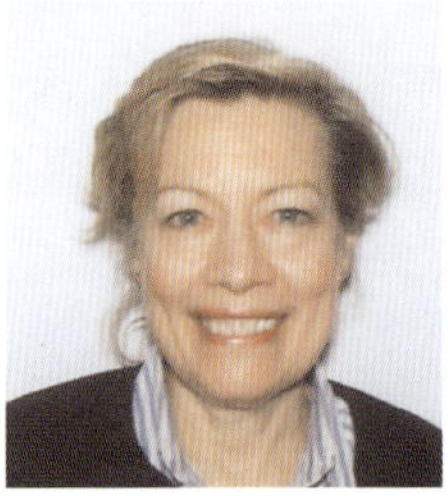

Acknowledgements

A work such as this can only reach its present state via the helpful critiques and comments by many friends and colleagues. Input from Donald Kuspit influenced the shape of this book. He spoke with me after reading the chapter on Walter Benjamin and strongly urged me to center the argument on my own work. He pointed out that every artist has a lineage and just as Brice Marden and modernist art are parts of mine, so too are the Asian and Aboriginal perspectives that I have observed and that have influenced my thinking. Therefore four of the chapters explain the evolution of my work and situate it in relationship to the metonymic process that I believe to be important now. One of these chapters describes my experience of the World Trade Center disaster and how it affected my painting. Other chapters demonstrate how the metonymic mode might be applicable to the work of a number of contemporary Western artists, such as Agnes Martin, Joseph Beuys and Brice Marden.

In the writing of this manuscript Kate Duncan was a constant guide and helpful editor. Her most salient message concerned the use of the pronoun 'I'. Strike it out and find another way of saying it, she said, cautioning me that wanting to become a writer takes a person on a long and perilous journey. But she inspired me to put words on paper, and to keep writing. My husband, Francis Claps, was always there as a safe haven.

I am indebted to my editor, Jenny Zimmer, for her constant advice and support, and to Brian Sadgrove for his inspired design for the book. A number of persons read the manuscript to assess its substance and style at various stages along the way. I am grateful for comments from Richard Vine, Irving Sandler, Laura Murray Cree, Jill Immerman, Ashley Crawford, and Carolina Rosensztroch. I also profited from comments by Dr. Konrad Oberhuber, Dr. Lorand Hegyi, Tom Bishop, Anne Kirker, Leighton Longhi, Amy Routman, Colby Collier, Ellen Handler Spitz and Anand Sarabhai. Special thanks are due to Betsy Brennan, Penelope Jaffray and Keith McConnell for their guidance and input. I would also like to acknowledge the assistance of Anthony Wallis of the Aboriginal Artists' Agency, Sydney.

Several chapters have been published previously in art journals. 'Painterly Thought and the Unconscious' was published in *Art Press*, Paris; the Greenberg essay first appeared as 'Painting Post Greenberg' in *Art Monthly Australia*; 'Viewing Walter Benjamin within a Global Perspective' appeared in *A Graduate Journal of Contemporary Art Criticism* and 'Affinities with Joseph Beuys' was included in the catalogue that accompanied my retrospective exhibition at the Saarland Museum in Saarbrucken, Germany. The Robert Motherwell interview was undertaken at Hunter College, New York.

I wish to gratefully acknowledge the artists whose interviews and art works are reproduced in this book and those individuals and art institutions who have provided the illustrative material.

Finally, I thank Anthony Bond, Suzi Gablik and Dr. Dieter Ronte for their perceptive understanding and contributions to the book.

Denise Green, 2005

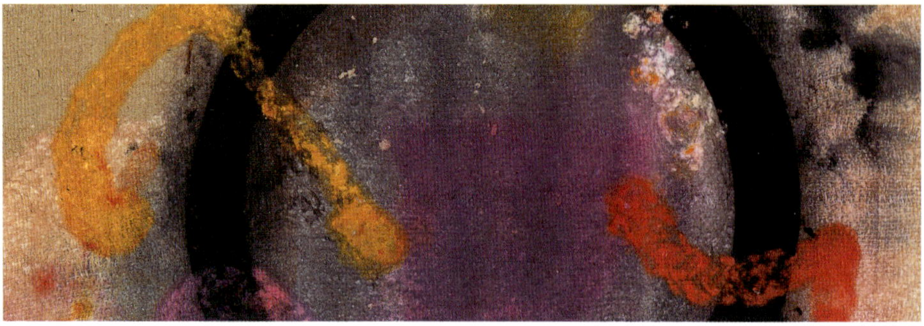

Introduction

An Alternative Paradigm

While completing the chapters and preparing to write an Introduction for this book I realized that one of the factors that motivated me to embark on this project was the discovery of Ramanujan's writings. Ramanujan was a folklorist and linguist on the faculty of the University of Chicago, a MacArthur Fellow, a leading poet in English in India and an important translator of medieval Indian poetry. He wrote a rich and profound analysis of what he saw as the difference between Western and Indian thought.

His key essay, *Is there an Indian way of thinking?,* was the result of a lifetime of reflection. But, to understand his text the reader needs a certain background in Western and Indian philosophical thought. It took me many years and numerous readings to penetrate the essence of Ramanujan's essay. As I moved towards a greater understanding I realized he made it possible for Westerners to think about Indian art in an Indian way. His essay also threw new light on aesthetic ideas in contemporary Western art.

At first I was immediately impressed by the way Ramanujan began his analysis by reference to Plato, Hegel and Kant – before referring to the Indian philosopher and lawmaker, Manu. Later, I realized he was constantly comparing their approaches, seeing Western philosophers from the perspective of Indian philosophers, and vice versa. For me, as a Westerner, it was shocking to learn that in India there is no

Denise Green, *Surya Chandra 1* (detail), 1986. Collection: Museum of Modern Art, Sydney.

universal moral law. Rather morality, or *dharma*, depends completely on the social and personal context that a person occupies. It takes into account their relationships, the natures of the persons involved (including the subject's own nature), the place and the time, as well as the stage of life that the person has reached. Indians are known to say completely different things on the same topic to different persons, depending on the relationship they share.

What struck me about Ramanujan's formulation of Indian aesthetics was that poetry, unlike the 'poetic' in Western aesthetics, does not proceed by metaphors. Instead, the human and natural world are intrinsically related to one another. I liked and understood Ramanujan's use of the linguistic term, metonym, which he used to explain a poem about a man and a clear-water shark in which the two figures are part of one scene, existing separately yet simulating each other.[1] This is a metonymic view of man in nature, where man is continuous with the context in which he finds himself and where nature and culture are not opposed to each other. Rather they are parts of the same continuum. Within this culture, to describe the landscape is to inscribe the character.

Ramanujan goes on to explain that container-contained relations are to be discovered in many images and concepts. Poems play with concentric containments. Indian literary texts are not structured according to a linear narrative, as in Western poems and novels, instead they are non-linear and non-sequential and each story *inside* the text illuminates the *outside*. From this explanation I derived an image that spoke to me as an artist. Concepts presented in Indian poetry and the ancient texts are based on concentric nests of ideas. The stepwells described in the fourth chapter of this book are an architectural manifestation of this aesthetic of concentric containment.

Houses are containers *par excellence.* Ramanujan states that in Indian culture a house can contribute to the fortune and pre-occupations of its occupants. In Ramanujan's terms the house is infused with properties whose mood and character extend to the persons inside and they become metonyms for one another. I realized that similar metonymic thinking was present in my own work. Chapter three describes how I developed an image of a house in which I had lived and which mirrored my inner state.

Ramanujan also addresses the idea of how space and time have different densities and properties. Different hours of the day are auspicious and other hours are inauspicious. In this way of thinking, units of time have properties that affect politics and religion and even breed certain kinds of maladies. Arts that are dependent on time, such as music, are subject to time's changing moods and properties. Ragas were generally only played at certain times of the day or during certain seasons. The making of a musical instrument is also sensitive to context. For example the gourd from which an instrument is made must be taken from a particular place and crafted by artisans of a particular caste, who observe particular austerities. These qualities of substance affect the quality of the instrument.

I realized that although Ramanujan's analysis offered a different way of thinking it had an application to the visual art of our period. Furthermore, thought of this kind seemed to be missing from the current discourse on contemporary Western painting. I also understood that his analysis was relevant for the technique of painting, which has tactile properties and is practised through gesture and the direct connection between hand and canvas. The conceptual framework for metonymic thinking may be Indian, but it is also close to my observation of Aboriginal culture, familiar to me because of my years growing up in Australia. Although Indian philosophy and thought has been in the West since the early nineteenth century, it is only within the last fifteen years that an Indian cognitive framework has been made known to Western thought through the writings of Ramanujan, Alan Roland and others.

My realization that Ramanujan's thought offered an explanation for certain characteristics of my work was followed by the recognition that I would have to write about my work myself if it were to be interpreted from this perspective. This led me to develop my ideas for this book. I began by challenging influential critics and critical attitudes in the art world that have a tendency to inhibit the understanding of painting today. For ten years my goal had been to write about Walter Benjamin's essay, *The Work of Art in the Age of Mechanical Reproduction*, but I was only able to achieve this after realising that Ramanujan's analysis functioned as an alternative paradigm. In critiquing Benjamin and Clement Greenberg I have been able to advance another aesthetic related to my experience as an artist and my present knowledge of Aboriginal and Asian cultures. Thus I introduce a different mode of thinking than that which is present in most Western art critical writing. My argument allows contemporary art to be interpreted from a broader, more global and pluralistic perspective.

The Self from a Global Perspective

In the writing of this book my most important guide and mentor has been Alan Roland, an astute psychoanalytic clinician and, importantly, an artist who himself has a deep knowledge and understanding of the creative process. Most relevant are the original insights he has developed by investigating the relationship between dreams and art (Roland, 1972 and 1981). He has published two major books from his research conducted in India and Japan. These develop a theoretical framework for a comparative, cross-cultural paradigm for better understanding of the self. When I talked with Alan about aesthetic processes that seemed metonymic, he introduced me to the work of Ramanujan. As I began to unravel the complexities of metonymic thinking, he pointed out that the configuration of the inner self varies significantly, depending on the subject's culture and its traditions. As examples, he referred to the configuration of the familial self of the Indian psyche, and contrasted it with the individualized self of Westerners. It is in the Indian familial self that the inner and outer is experienced metonymically, as a continuous entity rather than a duality. Therefore the fusion between self and art work tends to happen differently in Eastern and Western cultures.

Another motivating factor was my desire to argue for subjectivity in art. Discussions with Alan reinforced my ability to voice my point of view and affirm the basis of my expression to be in emotion. Throughout the last 45 years, non-objective painting that is rooted in subjectivity has been relegated to a cultural limbo in the discourse within the art world. In this book I explain how painting can function as a direct and tangible manifestation of inner states of consciousness.

Alan influenced my desire to better understand Aboriginal culture and its impact on me as an artist. His formulations of the Indian self as rooted in the invisible world, as well as the human, helped shape my perception that the self of the Aboriginal was part of a metonymic continuum that included the sacred beliefs of the people, the sanctity of special features of the landscape, and the use of materials. During my early years growing up in Brisbane I was drawn to Aboriginal culture and saw many ancient bark paintings and artefacts in the Queensland Museum. There are many different styles of Aboriginal painting, but my strong preference was for the bark paintings made by the indigenous people from Groote Eylandt. In these, the emphasis is metonymic. I left Australia before the new wave of art making in the 1970s, when contemporary

Aboriginal artists began synthesizing their traditional designs with modernist ideas.

The Chapters

This is a book of essays addressing the ideas that inform my work and thinking about art. In part, it is an outcome of my struggle to state the importance and relevance of subjectivity in painting. The book interweaves aspects of my own evolution as an artist, my comments on other artists and critiques of the work of two of the most important art critics of the middle twentieth century whose influence is still felt.

In four of the chapters I write about my early years in New York in the 1970s and of the evolution of my work since then. Some people may question the relevance of critiquing Walter Benjamin and Clement Greenberg at this late point, so let me explain the impetus behind my efforts to tangle with their thinking. When I arrived in New York in the late 1960s Benjamin and Greenberg were considered to be two of the most important critics. They had both argued against subjectivity in painting and had played a major role in shaping the context of the art world at that time. This book is anchored by my arguments against these influential critics who have powerful living legacies which continue to this day. Their ideas limit the understanding of art because their approaches are from a singularly Western perspective. In recent years, with major thinkers like Ramanujan and Roland being able to span two worlds, it has become possible to spell out a conceptual framework for metonymic thinking. A major part of the book explores how other artists might be seen to share my approach and have, consciously or unconsciously, incorporated modes of metonymic thought in the creation of their work.

The first chapter, *Some Limitations of Clement Greenberg's Writings: Referencing Aboriginal Vision*, explains how Greenberg believed in the historical inevitability of abstraction and argued against literary subject matter and illusionistic effects.
He defended painting that remained true to its medium, as pure form and colour. His approach was based on Western philosophical assumptions and its legacy in America has encouraged the belief that painting should speak for itself. Explanations about an artist's intentions or any underlying meanings were not endorsed by Greenberg. From my perspective, the abstract dimension of a painting is metonymically integrated with an inner reality – as is found in Aboriginal art works. The contemporary art world is nowadays being transformed by artists who combine influences from different cultural

and aesthetic traditions into the multi-faceted selves manifested in their works.

The second chapter, *A Critique of Walter Benjamin from a Globalist Perspective*, outlines how Benjamin's theory established a bifurcation between photography/film and painting. He dismissed painting on account of its 'aura' and defended mechanically reproduced works because they could help produce social change. But his critique was based on the assumption that the characteristics of the aura – such as tradition, ownership, the painting's use as an object of ritual and the viewer's contemplative relationship to the art work – are all external to the art object itself. I argue that Benjamin's approach is based on Western assumptions of progress, linearity and rationality and I strive to provide alternative viewpoints regarding the aura – by attempting to see it, for instance, from an Indian perspective that also sheds light on contemporary painting.

In the following chapter I begin to explore how other artists incorporate metonymic thinking in their work. *The Impact of Joseph Beuys*, interprets his art from the perspective of an Eastern cognitive framework. It was the presence of Beuys in New York in 1974 that triggered the introduction of symbolic imagery within my work. What my work shares with the work of Beuys is the reference to objects which have both mundane and transcendent qualities. Another affinity is that we both resonate with traditional cultures – Nordic and Germanic mythology and Central Asian societies for Beuys and, in my case, the Etruscan civilization and Aboriginal culture. Metonymic thinking is present in all these traditional cultures to which we have both been attracted.

I then proceed to write about my early years in New York and the establishment of a working aesthetic and its development over a thirty-year period. The next two chapters explore how my approach is shared by other artists who incorporate metonymic thinking in their work. Chapter four describes how in the 1970s my work developed through contact with Mark Rothko, Joel Shapiro, Ralph Humphrey and Joseph Beuys. I was involved in a battle to stay becoming a painter when the most advanced artists were making conceptual art, but I also enjoyed a close association with radical intellectual groups centered around *Semiotexte(e)*. During this period the key images of my painting vocabulary functioned as archetypes invested with personal meaning. Some of the works were included in a major show at the Whitney Museum, *New Image Painting*, which brought together a new generation of painters.

Chapter five is based on an interview with Robert Motherwell in which he talks about his relationship with Rothko. It is an intimate discussion of Rothko's character, including his secretiveness, his sense of ritual and his shaman-like qualities. Motherwell makes observations about the art world of the 1950s and discusses Rothko's early years and how his attitudes were shaped.

The sixth chapter describes how an initial encounter with India inspired my use of colour. On two subsequent visits, sponsored by the Sarabhai family, I made handmade paper works at the Gandhi Ashram Papermill. This helped me to distil the colour in my studio work. After returning to New York I came to understand my experiences in Asia through the writings of Ramanujan and Alan Roland. An interview with Brice Marden explores the way he was inspired by the dimension of *ch'i* which is conveyed in Chinese calligraphic writing.

Then, in 1992, my work changed abruptly. The colour dropped out of my paintings and during a five-year period the palette was limited to black and white. In this and a later body of works the use of paint became more direct, combining both symbolic and metonymic processes. This alternative paradigm and the development of an aesthetic attitude for the 1990s is the subject of the seventh chapter.

Chapter eight, *Painterly Thought and the Unconscious*, explores how other artists have handled sudden changes in their work. This emerged from my own experience in the 1990s when my formerly highly colouristic paintings suddenly shifted to black and white. This startling change was based on the integration of an emotional experience which had occurred twenty years earlier and which was still an unconscious force in my life. It proved to be evidence of a metonymic mode of thinking. I questioned Alex Katz, Frank Stella, Dorothea Rockburne and Barry Le Va about how changes had occurred in their work. They are artists whose thinking allows for leaps, intuitions and premonitions.

The final chapter, *Seeing the Attack: 11 September 2001*, describes my witnessing the terrorist attack on the World Trade Center in New York from my studio window nearby. The trauma evoked a new image in my paintings. In the aftermath, I continue working to develop the double meaning of the imagery. It references the twin towers as well as the scene of a childhood trauma.

I hope that these reflections will be of some value to the many who are engaged in exploring and interpreting the visual arts.

Notes

1 This excerpt from the poem, *What his concubine said about him*, illustrates how the landscape represents the character of the man:

> You know he comes from
> Where the fresh-water shark in the pools
> Catch with their mouths
> The mangoes as they fall, ripe
> From the trees to the edge of the field.
> At our place
> He talked big.

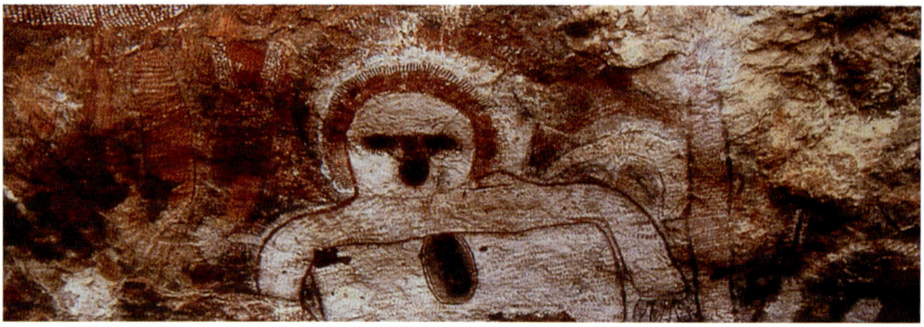

Chapter **1**

Some Limitations of Clement Greenberg's Writings: Referencing Aboriginal Vision

Clement Greenberg was one of the major art critics of the twentieth century and his ideas have great influence to this day. He wrote his most important essays for the *Partisan Review* in the 1940s. Focusing on developments within Western culture from the nineteenth century onwards, he articulated a theory that defended Modernism and avant-garde culture. One of his key arguments was that art should be intrinsic to itself, purged of social and political intentions. He favored painting as pure form and colour that remained true to its medium. In the late 1930s his contact with Hans Hofmann led him to argue for an exclusive focus on the formal values of painting. His critical stance was based on an assumption of the historical inevitability of abstraction. Greenberg played a major role in supporting the breakthroughs of the Abstract Expressionists. His significance as a critic is related to his establishment of a way of reading their work.

What are Greenberg's major ideas that have so affected the art world today? In one of his earliest and most important essays, *Towards a Newer Laocoon*,[1] written in 1940, Greenberg voiced many of the central concerns of his critique and argued in favor of abstract art, pure form and the purity of the medium.

Anonymous, *Wandjina Figure*, Australian Aboriginal rock painting, Napier Range, Kimberley, Australia.

If painting is to be pure, it has to be autonomous and independent of other art forms. According to Greenberg, up until the mid-nineteenth century, within Western culture, literature was the dominant art form. Post-Renaissance painters used illusionist effects to achieve a sense of tunneling into the picture surface so that it functioned as a window on a scene. In Greenberg's view, this served to convey literary subject matter. But, gradually the avant-garde moved painting towards its pure essence – with each generation eliminating more and more of the illusionistic effects in favor of intentional flatness. Implicit in his stance is a belief in the avant-garde with its promise of a radical renewal. He stated that, 'major art is impossible, or almost so, without a thorough assimilation of the major art of the preceding period'. In other words, each advance in painting should be understood in terms of a reaction to previous development in art – a premise that allowed Greenberg to interpret the achievements of the Abstract Expressionists as a reaction to Cubism. The spontaneous and direct gesture in their paintings was seen as a struggle against Cubist composition and the confines of the picture's edge.[2]

Another of Greenberg's important ideas was based on the materiality of the medium. He believed an important advance was made in painting when Manet, through his 'insolent indifference' to the subject matter, shifted focus toward the more physical qualities of the medium. Great energy entered his work through the risks he took in breaking pictorial conventions and allowing the painting to restrict itself to paint. Greenberg claimed that when the emphasis shifts to the medium, painting defines itself exclusively in terms of abstract values such as pure form and paint. 'The picture exhausts itself in its physical sensation', he said. 'There is nothing to identify, connect with or think about.'

Summarizing the evolution in painting from the seventeenth century on, he argued that until 1848 painting had dealt with literary themes and poetic effects through illusionistic devices. Only when avant-garde painters such as Courbet set out to convey what the eye saw rather than what the mind had been taught – such as idealized scenes – did they turn away from literary subject matter. Painting then became increasingly a matter of pure form and the physical nature of the medium. According to Greenberg, for avant-garde painting to achieve its essence as pure painting its prime task was to free the medium. Tracing the advances made by avant-garde painting over 100 years, among them the abandonment of such conventions as chiaroscuro and shading by modelling, he noted cogently, 'brushstrokes were defined for their own sake and primary colours replaced tone and tonality. Line became a third colour between two other colour areas'. From these observations,

Greenberg laid out the agenda for 'formalist' painting. His theory originated a critical attitude that shaped the reading of abstract art that continues into the present.

Although Greenberg's influence may not be directly felt in many exhibitions of contemporary art today, his legacy still commands a wide adherence. On the premise that modern abstraction in the twentieth century was self-referential and reductive, in other words, based on pure form and paint, it could only develop according to its own internal logic. By focusing exclusively on formal values in painting he encouraged the belief among critics, curators and some artists that painting should speak for itself. Explanations about intent or underlying meanings were no longer seen to be useful. Greenberg's vision still lives on through critics and curators assimilating his way of reading abstract art. His point of view has generated such acceptance that Greenberg continues to be one of the most influential critics of the last century.

At this point I would like to refer to the globalist perspective outlined in my next chapter. Greenberg, like Walter Benjamin, based his critique on Western philosophical assumptions and observations of Western art. An example of this is the assumption of a linear, historical evolution. Viewers today, armed with a global perspective, have acquired a new context and different ways of looking at art. Unlike Greenberg, they can often recognize evidence of a metonymic mode of thinking which is more explicitly present in Asian and Aboriginal art than in Western culture.

Let me cite as an example an Aboriginal art work called *A Map of Groote Eylandt*. This painting on bark is by an unknown artist and dates from 1948. It shows a simple centered image on a black background. The shape is outlined by a free-flowing white line and filled with a pattern of cross-hatched, broken and dotted lines. Bark paintings in this style are unique to Groote Eylandt, and found only during the 1940s and 1950s.

As an artist trained in the Western tradition, I could consider this bark painting to be an aerial map of Groote Eylandt, or, from a Greenbergian perspective, as a totally abstract design. But, through my research into Aboriginal art, I know it is much more than either. It is a sacred design that tells a 'Dreaming', or ancestral story.

According to Aboriginal beliefs, the features of a landscape bear the imprint of ancestral beings who moved across the land. Wherever they camped or performed some action, they left part of their spiritual essence metamorphosed into the shape of an island, a rock, or a tree.[3] Although the bark painting resembles an aerial view of

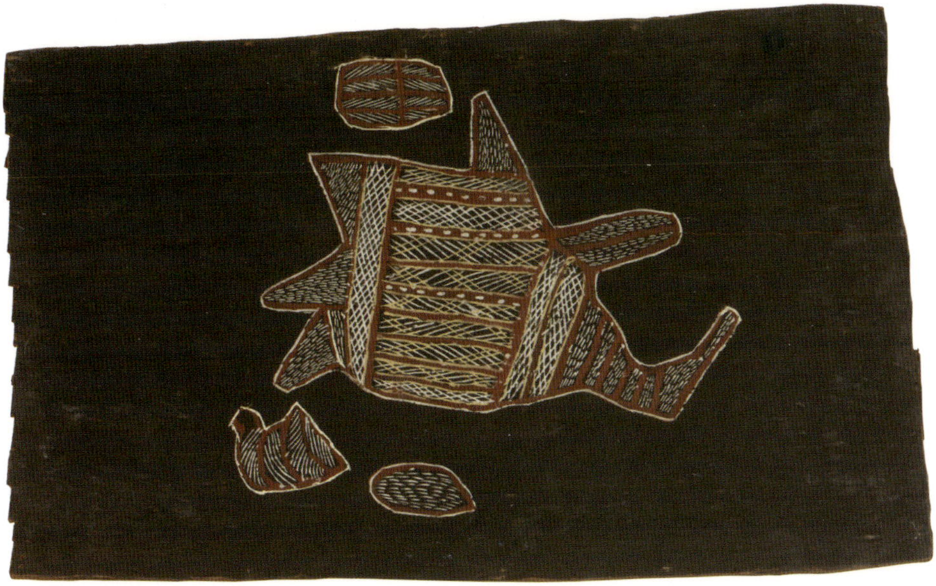

Unknown artist, *Map of Groote Eylandt*, c. 1948. Natural pigment on bark, 57.1 x 94 cm. Purchased 1959. Collection: Art Gallery of New South Wales. © Anindilyakwa Land Council. Photograph: AGNSW.

the island, for the Aborigines it also maps – with the intimate knowledge peculiar to hunters and fishermen – the island itself, where every material feature embodies the spiritual qualities of a mythological past and present. In other words, the Dreaming is always present, both in the artist's work and in the land itself.

As Aboriginal art works became more familiar, I began to wonder how differently the Aboriginal artist's mind works in comparison with those of Western artists. In the Western tradition, where emphasis has been placed on symbolic representation through figurative depiction, artists have followed a dualistic mode of thought, rooted in Cartesian philosophical assumptions. The formal purity of abstraction which Greenberg championed, with its change from forms representing symbolic depiction to those that are autonomous, is similarly dualistic in its thinking. By contrast, Aboriginal and Asian artists usually follow a metonymic mode of thinking, which implies a monistic framework. Traditionally, in Eastern philosophy, there are no dualities established between mind and body or spirit and matter, instead they belong to the same monistic continuum.[4] For example, in Indian thinking, mind and body are both considered to be matter, mind being subtle matter and the body a grosser manifestation of matter – but they share the same continuum. For the artist, metonymic thinking implies that an art work is the direct manifestation of the artist's state of consciousness.[5]

If I introduce this linguistic reference it is because metonymic thinking has become an integral part of a conceptual framework I have evolved in trying to understand the Aboriginal way of working and also the maturing of my own creative process. It is the only word that fits the reality of what I am trying to describe. Metonymic thinking implies the fusion of the inner spiritual and outer material world. When artists create metonymically, the outward aspects of the art work are seamlessly connected with the inner state of the artist – as in the bark painting of Groote Eylandt. By contrast, when Western artists express their inner vision in symbolic or abstract, formalist terms there is an implied separation between themselves and the art work. The art work is rarely, if ever, talked about in terms of the artist's inner state of mind.

But how do Aboriginal artists express this fusion? To begin with, the self of the Aboriginal extends into mythic and mystical realms that are collectively shared. This is in stark contrast to the experience of most Western artists. More concretely, Aboriginal artists use calligraphic markings that are metonymically infused with the power of myth and ritual enactment. Painted on bark or stone, or on their own bodies, these markings externalize spirituality into an object which then becomes sacred.[6] On the other hand, although Western religious art may have been influenced by the artist's spiritual beliefs and experiences, the critical discourse it generates generally does not refer to the altarpieces, crucifixion scenes or Madonnas as sacred objects.

Artists working today in our culture sometimes use a metonymic way of thinking, but I would like to emphasize important difference between the way Western and Aboriginal artists use the process. In the best Aboriginal art, the inner world of the artist belongs to a mythic consciousness that is also sacred and shared. The essence of their metonymic thinking is that the markings, the inner state of the artist and the mythic are all of one piece. This is why the art work becomes sacred. It is not only the subject that is sacred, but the art object itself becomes sacred.

For Western artists metonymic thinking usually conveys experiences other than religious ones. Further, the metonymic fusion between inner self and the art work can only be expressed intuitively through different uses of the medium. My painting has

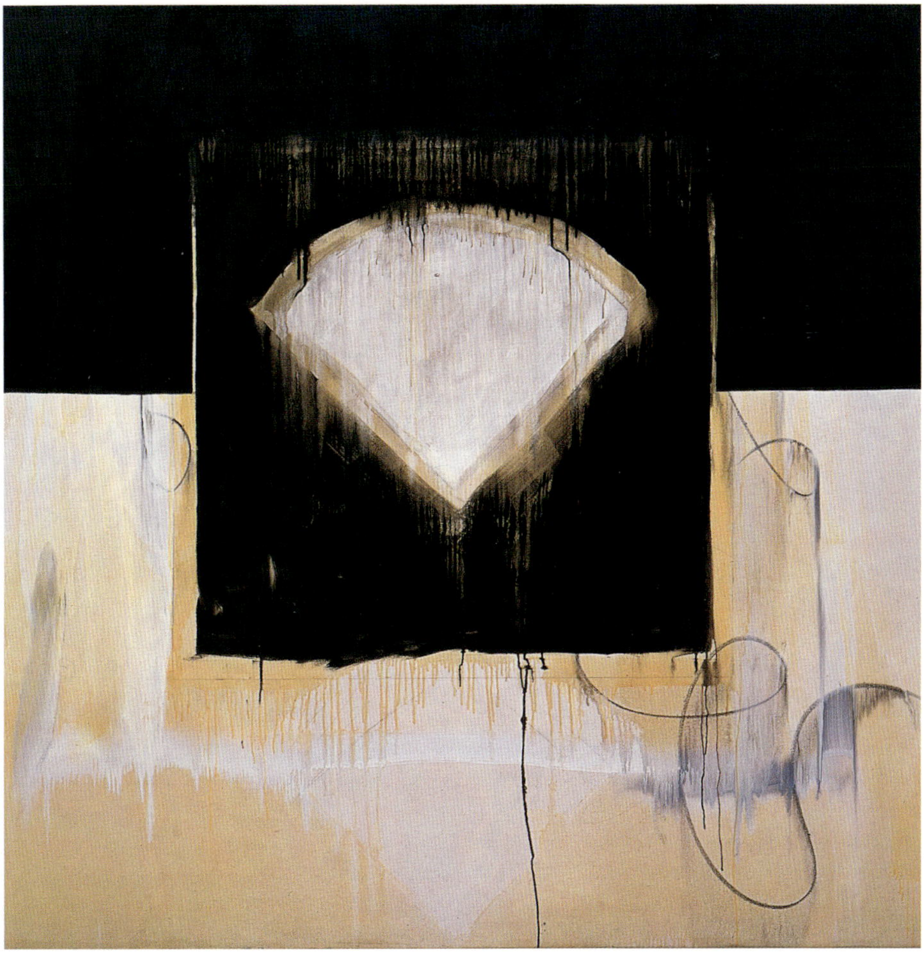

often been described as expressionistic, but there is no conscious intent to tell a story about my emotions. Rather the impulse and gestural brushwork in my paintings allow for the manifestation of an inner state of mind. To think about my work metonymically is to understand that the abstract dimension of the painting is integrated with an inner reality. Rather than by the development of shapes, it is the different ways of handling the paint that allow a Western artist's subjectivity to fuse with the work.[7] This crucial dimension is ignored in Greenberg's critical theory.

Greenberg and those who followed him failed to recognize that abstract artists

Denise Green, *Taxes*, 1994. Oil on canvas, 178 x 178 cm. © Solomon R. Guggenheim Museum, New York. Photograph: Ellen Labensky.

working today in Western culture sometimes use a metonymic way of thinking not altogether unlike that of the Aboriginal artists of Groote Eylandt. For example, Agnes Martin's early paintings are monochromatic grids. More recently she has worked with horizontal or vertical bands of colour. Yet her paintings have been discussed only as abstractions without alluding to their expressiveness. In a recent interview, she spoke to Irving Sandler about the references to nature in her work: 'My work is non-objective like that of the Abstract Expressionists. But I want people, when they look at my painting, to have the same feelings they experience when they look at landscape, so I never protest when they say my work is like landscape. But it's really about the feeling of beauty and freedom that you experience in landscape'.[8]

Her feelings for nature and her emotions are conveyed by means of the process she uses to draw the grids. The straight lines are not mechanically made but have the kind of fluctuations and imperfections we find in nature. These fluctuations, along with the rhythms established by the regular patterns of rectangles, imbue her work with a sense of exaltation, and maintain the connectedness between her inner state of tranquillity and her ideas about happiness and beauty.

Ross Bleckner's paintings are also commonly understood as abstractions. In a recent catalogue essay, Mark Rosenthal claims that Bleckner has a paradoxical approach to abstraction because he incorporates stylistic aspects of op art into his work.[9] Bleckner's subjects and motifs range from optically dizzying stripes to nocturnal landscapes, chandeliers, funerary urns and abstract constellations of dots. Yet, in an interview I did with Bleckner, he said that his imagery often comes from his experience of nature. He said: 'I actually remember driving down a highway in the wintertime when there were no leaves on the trees and seeing the sun set really low in the back of the trees. The pattern, intensity, verticality and the strobe of the sun was so fascinating because it was both an image and a landscape and it became this whole other thing. Because of its density and light it became almost cinematic. And that became an idea for a painting.'[10] 'The work for me', he added later, 'is just a vehicle to explore the idea of spirituality. There's a sense of imagery that I'm drawn to. I know what kind of art historical terms it would be predicated on. In general it's images of ascension, rhapsody, episodic, meaning, epiphany, which always lead to endings – which is the apocalyptic thing. If the images are in the paintings they become theatrical, like Caravaggio's or El Greco's. They're always images of light'.

Agnes Martin, *Night Sea*, 1963. Oil and gold leaf on canvas, 182.9 x 183.9 cm. Private collection. Courtesy of Pace Wildenstein Gallery, New York.

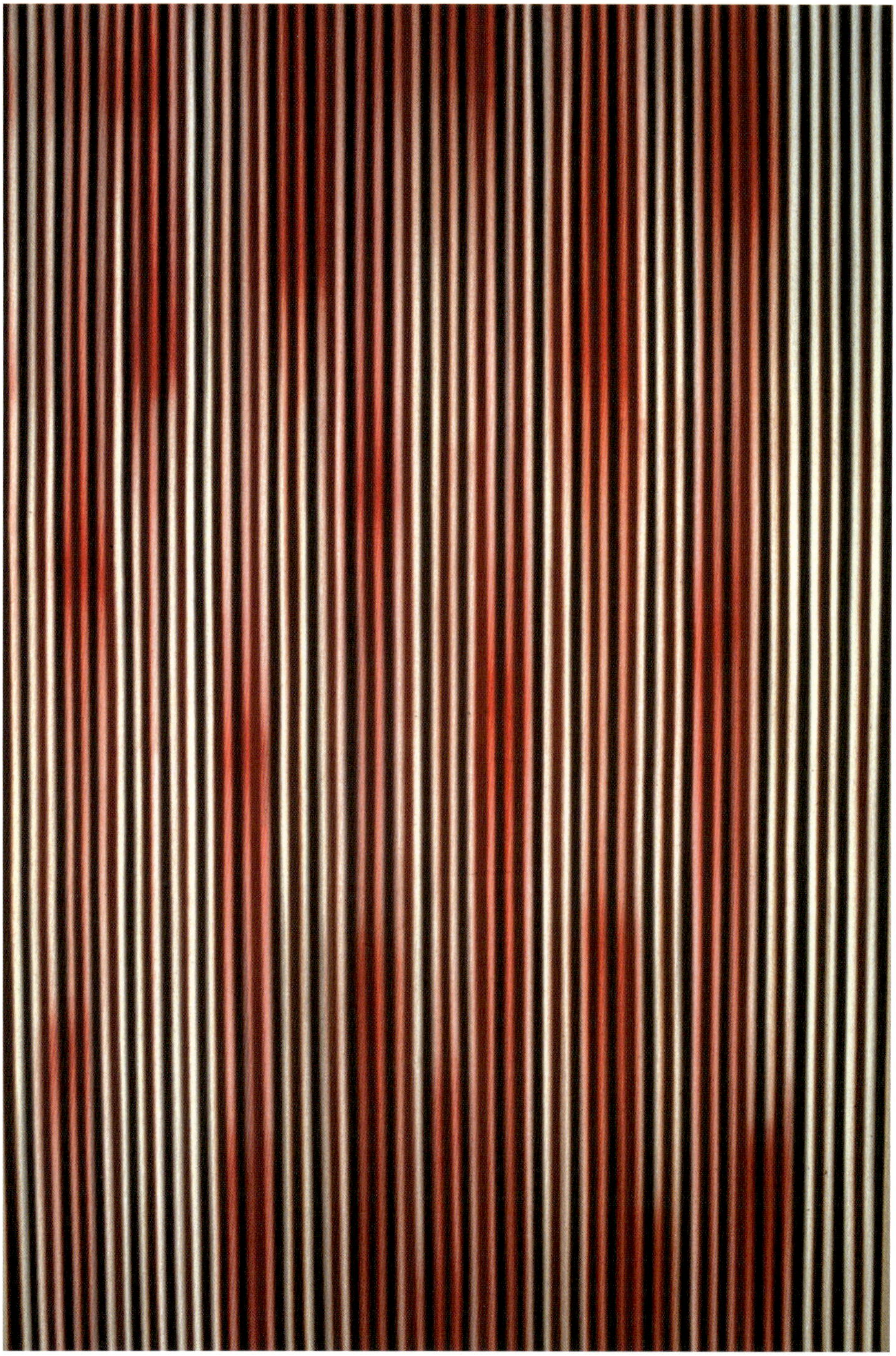

Rose Bleckner, *Burning Trees*, 1986. Oil on canvas, 270 x 178 cm. Courtesy of the Artist.

Bleckner's painting *Burning Trees* (1986) appears totally abstract, but the dizzying stripes are not simply a simulation of an early abstract style. He aspires to evoke an idea of spirituality in his work and conveys this metonymically through images of light. But Mark Rosenthal, in his catalogue essay, appears to ignore these references. He fails to take into account the inner motivation of the artist. This leads him to dismiss the whole notion of self.

Metonymic thinking in art implies that one must take into account the inner world of the artist. This is something that Greenberg and his adherents have ignored, yet it is just this inner state of mind that can be metonymically conveyed in a painting. To further this idea, we must be aware that the self of the artist can differ significantly according to culture, tradition and the individual. Western artists structure their inner selves to attain unique identities. This encourages innovation in the visual expression of what concerns each artist. They access different sides of the self, both conscious and hidden, through a process of intuitive visual thinking. Although it is not a verbal or rational process, every painter invents a personal language that gives outward form to an inner state of feeling.

In the traditions of Aboriginal and Asian societies, the inner self is communally and/or transcendentally based, and artists aspire to evoke spiritual and other states of consciousness in the viewer. In Aboriginal culture the self is also connected to the sacred space of the landscape. Artists are custodians of the myths that are associated with a sacred site and they use a secret set of designs or calligraphic markings that manifest the sacredness of the space. These designs or markings do not function as symbols, instead they are like mantras, invested with sacred power. The efficacy of the sacred is lost if the markings change. Only those who belong to the culture, or those who are in tune with the religious beliefs and social context of these cultures, can understand the significance of the imagery. Even then, outsiders would not necessarily have the same experience in responding to the paintings. It depends on an interchange between the selves of artist and viewer as to how we respond to either Aboriginal or Western art.

Although Greenberg's analysis was limited to the Western tradition of painting, it contributed a valid and accurate commentary on the art of his time. However, he could not appreciate that by expressing an inner state of mind, painters could begin to have much in common with artists from radically different traditions. Neither he nor his adherents could address the issue of a synthesis between modernist and non-Western ideas in the work of many contemporary artists. The situation today is different from the early part of the twentieth century when Picasso and the Cubists were influenced by the sophisticated formal qualities of African masks and sculptures. These artists incorporated the formal aspects of tribal art into their own work, but African art works are more than just volumes, lines and planes. In their own context, they have another level of significance because they are empowered with spiritual and magical properties. To what extent Picasso may have intuitively grasped the mystical meaning of certain African and Iberian sculptures is uncertain. But, within a Western context, his paintings cannot be considered as sacred or magical objects.

Today the contemporary art world is undergoing a transformation and must be interpreted from a broader, more global, and pluralist perspective. During the first decades of immigration to America different ethnic and national groups arrived, principally from Europe. It is only since the mid-sixties that immigrants from radically different cultures have come to the United States, with their own languages and varied spiritual, conceptual, religious and philosophic views. This opening up of a global horizon gives us a new vision of art which can be interpreted from different points of view. An art historian might say that within a given art work artists are combining influences from many different cultural and aesthetic traditions. This point of view is shared by curators such as Lorand Hegyi and Acilla Bonita Oliva who have introduced the notion of a personal diaspora. For them, an artist's language is integrated through their personal history of living in different cultures, rather than through purely formal means. In the literary world, too, it has become acceptable to see artists from the South Asian diaspora to the United States as combining their sensibilities with the new culture here. They develop a bicultural self which is manifest in their work.

Other critics might think that once-autonomous traditions with distinct languages are in fact being absorbed into a monoculture. From this perspective, these traditions seem more like various regional inflections or dialects of one contemporary art language.[11]

From the perspective of the diaspora phenomenon, artists who change cultures radically, yet remain both consciously aware of their cultural origins and accept their indigenous selves, can create artistic languages from their own personal subjective stories. In an interview with Hegyi, he referred to the large cities in the West where one

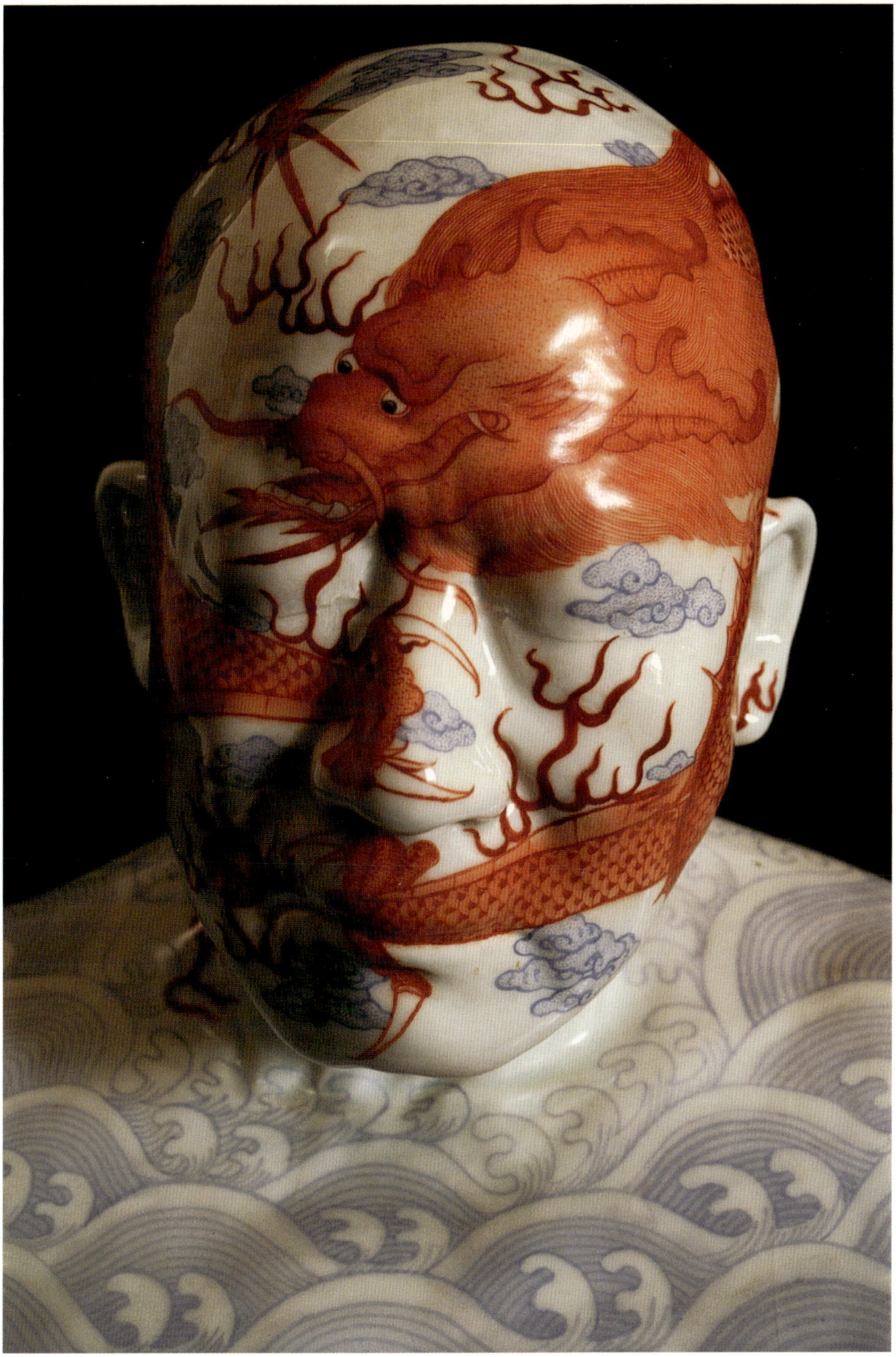

Ah Xien, *China China*, *Bust 36*, 1999. Porcelain in overglaze red and blue in dragon cloud and ocean design. 44 x 35 x 25 cm. Courtesy of the Artist. Collection: Mr John Silberman, New York.

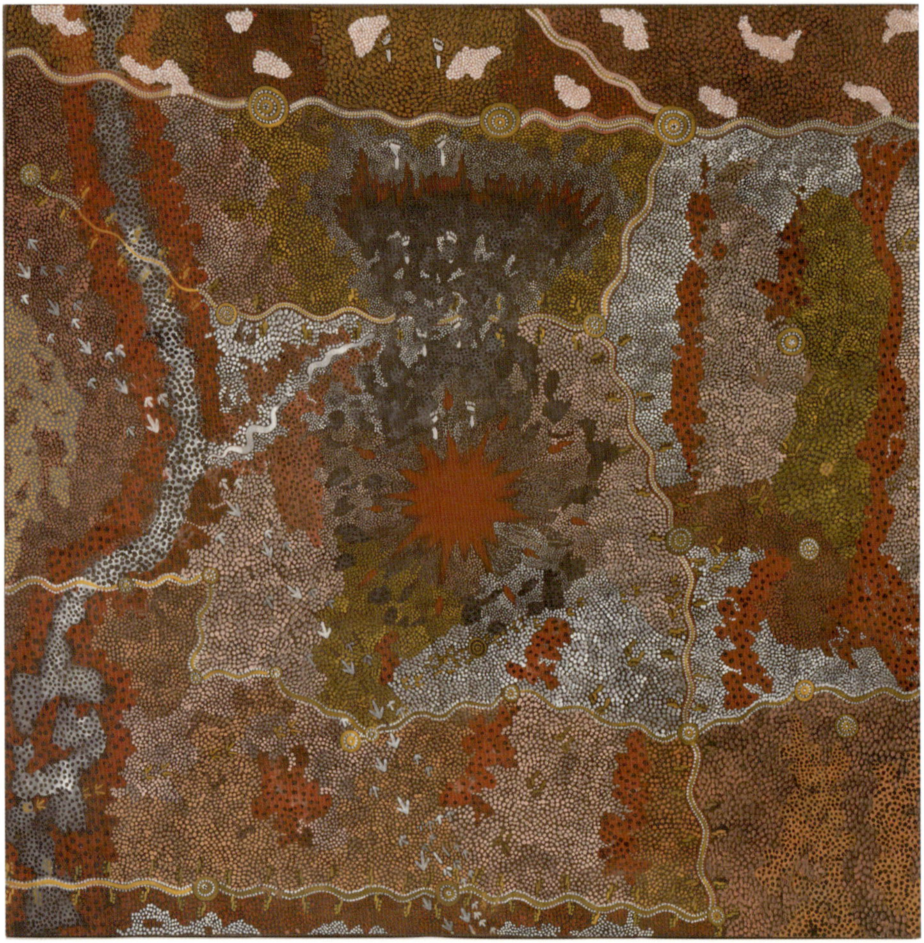

Clifford Possum Tjapaltjarri, Tim Leura Tjapaltjarri, Anmatyerre, Arrernte, Papunya, Alice Springs. *Warlugulong*, 1976. Synthetic polymer paint on canvas, 168.5 x 170.5 cm. Purchased 1981. Collection: Art Gallery of New South Wales, Sydney. ©Aboriginal Artists' Agency Ltd. Photograph: Christopher Snee for AGNSW.

finds the mixing of ethnic groups and the establishment of new kinds of artistic communication in which artists use their 'home languages' and remain connected to their origins.[12] But the 'home languages' are no longer vehicles of national identity. Instead, they are more personal stories of important moments in the artists' earlier biographies. As the artists move from their places of origin, their selves become like mosaics composed of stones from different cultures. This complexity becomes part of their language as artists. Within the experience of each stone there is a different story to recount. From Hegyi's perspective, the phenomenon of the personal diaspora is bound up with the problem of language, because diaspora means that basically what an individual possesses is not physical things, but rather a language which is created in establishing a personal and subjective story. This language can function in many different sociological forms. As a result, what we find is not so much a global language of art, but rather the countless individual languages that combine aspects of both indigenous and Western cultures and are set within a global context.

The implication of this situation for the art historian is that explanations about the production of art can no longer be confined within the frame of Western thinking. Instead, one must go to the source, to the artist, to understand what kind of thinking and configuration of the self has gone into a particular work. No canonic way of speaking about form can exist without being receptive to the hundreds of fine and defined references to the artist's original culture.

Although I have restricted my discussion here to traditional forms of Aboriginal art, there are also contemporary artists who are synthesizing these forms with Western modernist ideas in many innovative ways. For example, Clifford Possum Tjapaltjarri's paintings combine a number of mythological *Dreaming* or ancestral stories that are layered to form a complex network of *Dreaming* tracks. There is a parallel between this type of painting and European maps.[13]

The work of Ah Xian is an example of the Chinese diaspora to Australia. Ah Xian moved to Sydney twelve years ago, but the complexity of his background is part of his language as an artist. In the new context of Sydney he absorbed influences from the Western tradition of bust portraiture, which is largely absent from Chinese art. His vividly decorated busts combine these new elements with traditional Chinese porcelain ware designs.[14] These are not only formal elements, or superficially adapted forms, but an artistic language which is an integral part of his person.[15]

In a similar way, my own work combines elements from various cultural contexts. I came to New York from Australia, with its English colonial background and a Western educational system. Yet it differs from traditional Western societies because of the presence of the Aborigines and their ancient culture. It also has an important Asian element through immigration. The complexity of this background is part of my language as an artist. I then came to another context, New York, adopting further elements from the art world there, but seen through the filter of my origins and fusing them with my observations of Aboriginal art and my present understanding of its language. Traces of all these elements can be found in each of my paintings.

In the West, this mixing of cultures contributes to a different kind of world with complex individual positions. Because there is no one direction, no absolute compass with which to impose a single aesthetic ideal, globalism at the political and economic level will extend our capacity to accept an unlimited number of individual languages at the cultural level. Today, this is already understood and discussed in other fields such as anthropology, literature, filmmaking, music and cross-cultural psychology. Contemporary art will no longer be read within the critical framework established by Greenberg. Instead new frameworks will emerge in response to the phenomenon of multi-cultural artists who carry their own world within themselves as in a diaspora, and whose art works contain different modes of thinking and configurations of the self.

Notes

1 Clement Greenberg, 'Towards a Newer Laocoon', *Partisan Review 7*, no. 4 (July-August 1940), reprinted in Francis Frascina, (ed.), *Pollock and After: The Critical Debate*, Harper & Row, New York, 1985.

2 Greenberg also interpreted the large fields of colour in Newman's and Rothko's painting as a reaction against Cubism and the picture's edge as a confine.

3 According to Margo Neale, 'In traditional Aboriginal culture ... nature – in this case, the landscape of the artist's country – is depicted as a kind of three dimensional map. The actions of ancestral beings are indelibly imprinted in the shapes of natural features, the colourings, textures and the topographic dimensions. The land. like the paintings that represent it, is a map of ancestral journeys and events, a map of Dreamings'. Margo Neale, *Yiribana: An Introduction to the Aboriginal and Torres Strait Island Collection*, The Art Gallery of New South Wales, 1994.

4 Alan Roland, *In search of Self in India and Japan: Towards a Cross-Cultural Psychology,* Princeton University Press, 1988.

5 Although there is some notion of Abstract Expressionism expressing the artist's inner state of consciousness, the critical discourse has understood this work as a stylistic development in reaction to earlier developments in art, such as Cubism.

6 Margo Neale speaks of, '... the idea of spiritual power invested in works of artists in the form of myriad dots, cross-hatching or other optical effects', op.cit., p.10. Another example is of mantras performed in other cultures where the name of the god or goddess is repeated. These are not symbolic representations of the god or goddess, but contain their active power.

7 I would like to cite the example of the painting 'Taxes' and explain how it functions simultaneously as an abstraction and as a metonymic mode of my inner state of mind. This painting belongs to a group of black and white paintings I did in 1994. In these, instead of drawing with coloured paint sticks directly on the canvas as I usually had done, I used the paint in diluted washes so that it made drips and runs in subtleties of gray. As a result, my paintings became more expressive. It was only a year or so later, after completing ten of these large canvases, that I realized they expressed feelings of grief for my father who had died twenty years earlier. Although this work, which grew out of feelings of loss and absence, does not depict these emotions, it is the direct manifestation of my inner emotional state through the medium of the paint itself.

8 Agnes Martin interviewed by Irving Sandler, *Art Monthly (UK)* 169, September 1993, p. 13.

9 Mark Rosenthal, *Abstraction in the Twentieth Century: Total Risk, Freedom, Discipline*, Guggenheim Museum, New York, p. 69.

10 Ross Bleckner interviewed by Denise Green, in *Painterly Thought,* catalogue, Raab Gallerie Berlin, 1994.

11 I am indebted for this comment to Richard Vine, Managing Editor, *Art in America.*

12 Lorand Hegyi interviewed in conjunction with a panel discussion, 'Ethnic Minorities in the Artworld', Museum Moderner Kunst Stiftung Ludwig, Vienna, Austria, 1996.

13 Margo Neale, op.cit., p.64.

14 *China China: The Work of Ah Xian and Selections from the Rockefeller Collection,* presented at the Asia Society and Museum, 9 October 2002 to 9 February 2003.

15 While artists have incorporated different cultural traditions in painting – Rembrandt is an example of a seventeenth century Dutch Christian artist illustrating Hebrew mythology using Classical compositions, conventions and Italian techniques of perspective and chiaroscuro – they are all within the context of Western civilization. Today with the globalist diaspora, artists are combining cultural traditions from various civilizations based on radically different premises.

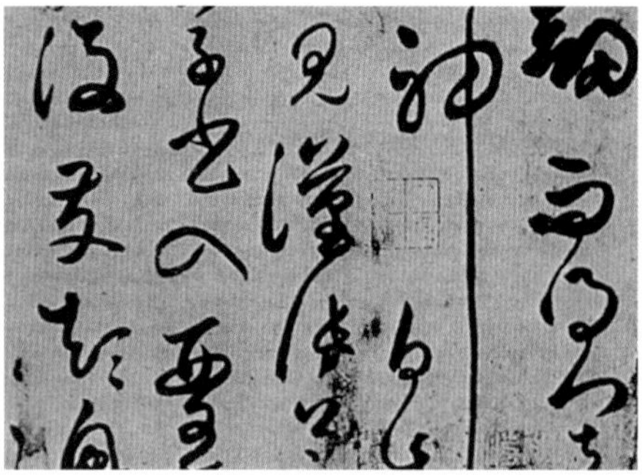

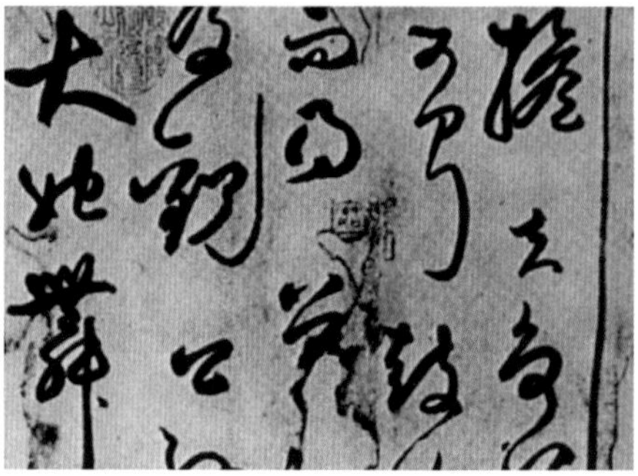

Chapter **2**

A Critique of Walter Benjamin from a Globalist Perspective

In the 1970s the legacy of Walter Benjamin in the art world left myself and other painters struggling to overcome a sense of invisibility. I am compelled to address Benjamin's ideas because his legacy adds to the crush of Western thought that shuts down the alternative patterns of aesthetic thinking that I am involved in. The barriers and prejudices that are in place, and that limit the understanding of painting, are in large part due to his enduring impact.[1]

Benjamin was an independent Marxist, a leading intellectual and literary critic writing in Germany in the 1930s, who was concerned with how cultural forces could produce social change. He believed that art should serve that purpose. He perceived that art based on mechanical reproduction could reach the masses and therefore he valued photography and film and dismissed painting. Photography and films are accessible to large audiences and can be viewed simultaneously in different places, whereas painting is only available to a limited few and is approached in a solitary and contemplative way. His ideas became influential in the art world in the mid-sixties when artists started incorporating photography and the moving image into their conceptually based practices. They turned to performance, video and conceptual art to critique the dominant culture and rejected painting on the basis of its elitism. His legacy continues to this day as his point of view permeates the cultural sphere that shapes those important segments of the curatorial and critical discourse that devalue the traditional art of painting.

Benjamin's system of thought was based on the bifurcation of the visual arts into two branches, painting and sculpture on the one hand, and photography and film on the other. The concept of the 'aura' is central to his theory of art and was the means by which he questioned the relevance of painting. He argued that the aura is only present in unique and original art works. His concept of the aura is multi-layered. In a key essay, *The Work of Art in the Age of Mechanical Reproduction*,[2] he presents four different characterizations of the aura. They are tradition, the viewer's contemplative relationship to the art work, ownership, and the art work as an object of ritual. These four facets of the aura are all external to the art object itself.

The first characterization of the aura is that paintings are embedded in an artistic and cultural tradition while at the same time perpetuating it. Because Benjamin laid such a weight on innovation, he therefore saw painting as a conservative force which interfered with progressive social change.

His second dimension of the aura is that unique and original art works have a power and presence, which demand that the viewer approach them in a contemplative state. It is implied that in this state the viewer undergoes an enrichment of the self. On the other hand, with mechanically reproduced art, the relationship of the viewer to the art work changes.[3] Benjamin focuses on mass responses to film and photography and how this affected individual responses. Furthermore, if these works had social content and were shown to a communal audience, they would 'stir' the viewers to political action. This would lead to a transformation of the whole society rather than of the individual self.

The third facet of the aura is the particular tradition of ownership. Unique art works and their aura have been owned by the élite, first the aristocracy and then the bourgeoisie, who thereby partook in their prestige. As a Marxist he believed in the redistribution of wealth from the bourgeoisie to the masses and the elimination of ownership. Art which at that time belonged to the bourgeoisie, he believed, should instead be in the hands of the masses. Since photography and film do not exist as unique originals, they therefore function outside the tradition of restricted ownership.

The fourth facet encompasses the ritual function of the aura. In his view, art works have their origin in ritual, magic and religion. But, since the Renaissance, the rituals

‘**The concept of *Ma*, or emptiness, is present in both Japanese and Chinese landscape painting. In most paintings it is conveyed by mist. In Western aesthetic terms emptiness would function as negative space in which forms do not exist, whereas in Eastern aesthetic terms, *Ma* is actually full of being.**’

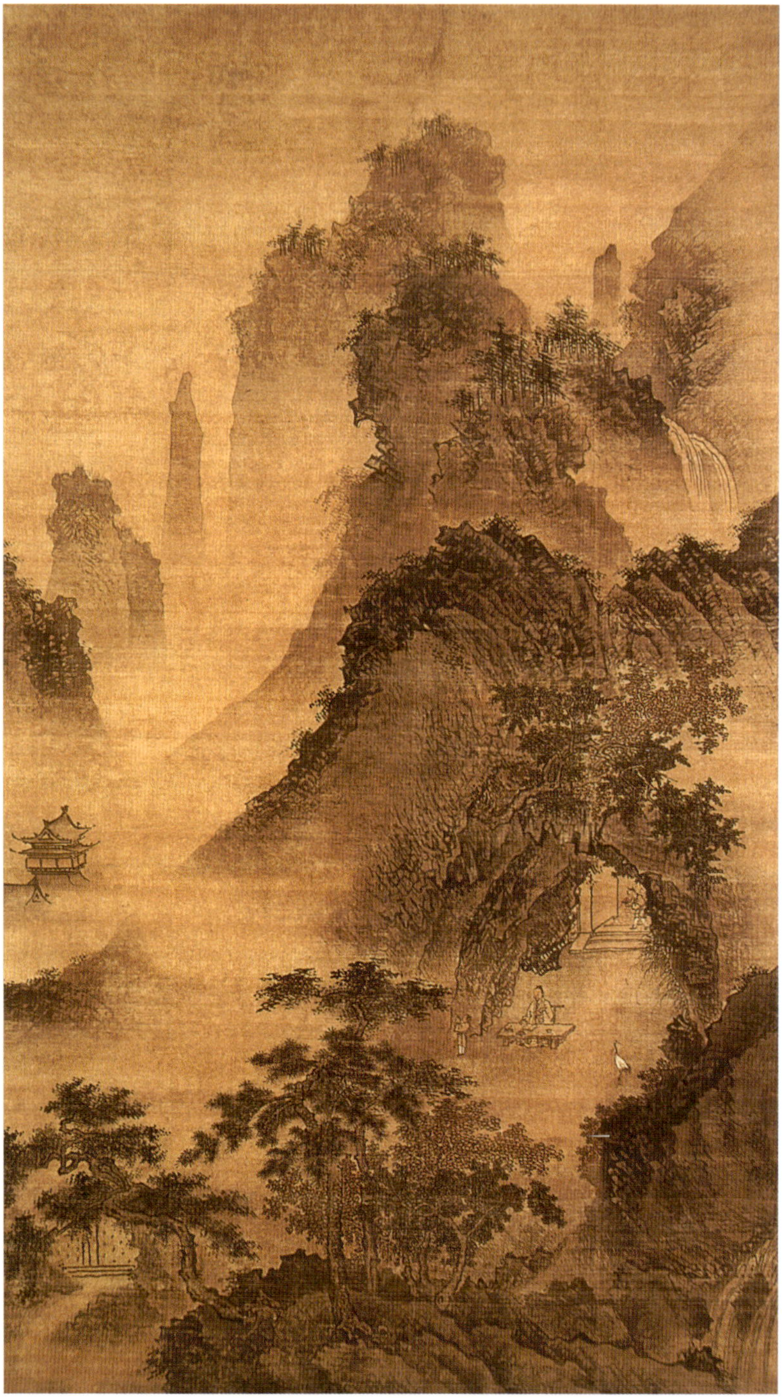

Anonymous (late Ming), *Studying 'The Classic of Change'*. Hanging scroll, ink and colour on silk, 180.3 x 103.7 cm. Collection: Shanghai National Museum.

became secularized in the 'cult of Beauty'. With the rise of socialism in the nineteenth century, art as ritual no longer seemed relevant to the masses. To the extent that mechanically reproduced art works had political content, then political change would, he believed, replace ritual as the function of art.[4]

Benjamin's way of thinking was poetic, associative and ruminative. But, even so, in his critical approach he subscribed to a linear view of history.[5] This view was grounded in an assumption of the historical inevitability of social progress and the concomitant evolution of art. For Benjamin, this evolution meant the gradual disappearance of unique art works with an aura, while films and photography would gain relevance and dominance. In his dialectical thinking, mechanically reproducible art would advance the cause of the proletariat and the proletariat would advance the use of mechanically reproducible art.[6]

Benjamin relied completely in his thinking on Western theories and writers, such as Hegel, Bertoldt Brecht and Rudolf Arnheim, among many others. What would have happened if Benjamin had possessed a more global perspective? There are different paradigms functioning in Eastern and Asian cultures and if Benjamin had taken into account these traditions, how would it have enabled him to see things differently? He might have relied on the theories of the Indian poet, linguist and folklorist A.K. Ramanujan and quoted the psychoanalysts Alan Roland and Akihisa Kondo. He could have referred to the metonymic thinking of the Australian Aboriginal artists of Groote Eylandt and the Kathakali dancers from Cochin in Southern India.[7] If he had been aware of the *Ma* concept in Japanese culture and the dimension of *ch'i* (breath), which is conveyed in Chinese calligraphic writing, it would have added to a more global view. I would like to outline some alternative viewpoints to each of the four facets of Benjamin's aura, but from my understanding of Asian and Aboriginal perspectives.

The first issues to consider are the roles of tradition and modernization in an ancient society like India. This will be very different from Benjamin's notion that focuses on innovation and tradition as being contradictions. According to Milton Singer, Indians use adaptive strategies to incorporate innovations into traditional patterns.[8] Technological changes are used in the service of tradition, which allows for continuity and change. For instance, Singer talks of a physical separation between workplace and home which symbolically occurs as a cultural difference. This means that at home Indians follow a traditional lifestyle, but at work they incorporate foreign innovations and adapt to a modern lifestyle. Yet rituals are still performed on modern machinery. In a culture that values ambiguity, both the modern and traditional lifestyles are lived and experienced without a sense of inconsistency.

Westerners, who live their life according to universal principles, would think of this as having a contradictory experience. But for Indians, proper behavior (or *dharma*) is acting according to the dictates of any given social context. Ramanujan refers to this as contextualization. The culture assimilates Western influences by assigning them to different contexts. In other words the culture imprints and patterns everything that enters it and turns all things, even enemies and rivals, inwards into itself.[9]

The next issue to consider is Benjamin's critique of the contemplative attitude to the art object and its aura. But he was using aura in a very different way because he was adopting a Sanskrit term without showing an understanding of the Hindu notion of it. In Hindu thinking, 'shakti' refers to the energy in the universe, which is in everything and anyone, animate or inanimate, and the aura is the physical manifestation of this energy in terms of its vibration and colour. Everyone and everything has a different level of consciousness and a different kind of aura. According to Hindu thinking, only very few individuals, those of a higher consciousness, can actually see the aura.

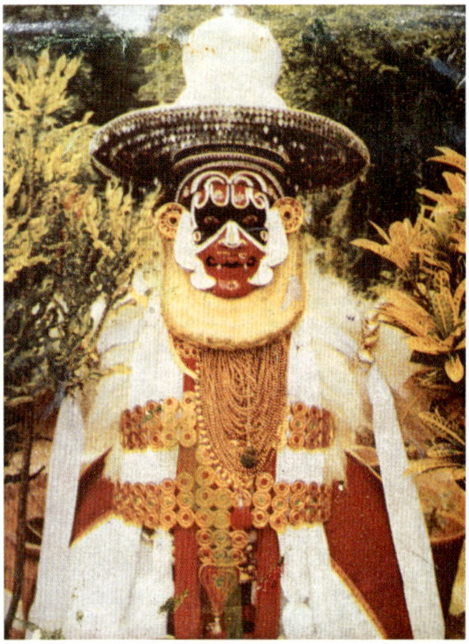

Anonymous, Kathakali Dancer. Colour photograph, Gurukulam Kathakali, Yogam, Cochin, India.

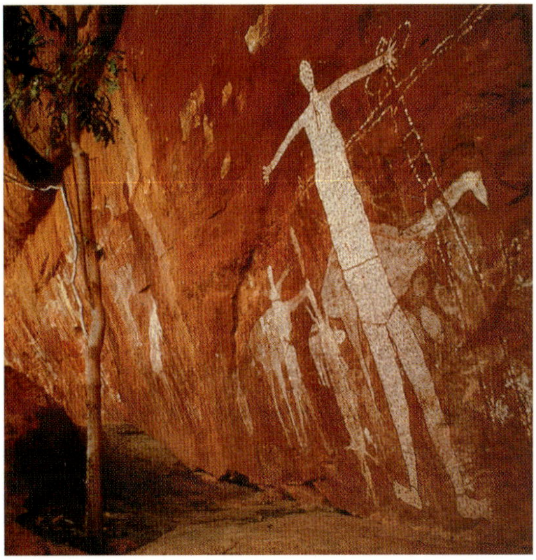

Anonymous *Quinkin Figure*, Australian Aboriginal rock painting, Queensland, Australia.

What are the implications of this non-Western notion of the aura with regard to our contemplative relationship to the object? From the Hindu standpoint, mechanically reproduced works, whether film or photographs, would also have an aura. The aura is intrinsic to all objects and the aura of any art work, including mechanically reproduced works, would be more or less powerful depending on the quality of the work. So, from an Asian perspective, in contrast to Benjamin's point of view, viewers would also approach film and photographs in a contemplative state of mind.

The third issue concerns the ownership of art. Benjamin wanted mechanically reproduced art to reach the masses because he believed it could contribute toward social change. In India, traditional art works, all of which have mythic and transcendent qualities, have been hand reproduced for centuries. Today, these works are machine reproduced and they still have their sacred meanings and manifestations. For example, most traditional homes have shrine rooms, with both statues and photographs of statues representing gods, goddesses and gurus. These rooms are reserved for worship and ritual, both by individuals and for the family worshipping together. Certainly, within this culture, some traditional art works, which also are reproductions, have a higher status and value because they are owned by an élite. But traditional art is owned by everyone. Hence, mechanically reproduced works carry forward and continue the tradition. From an Asian perspective tradition is not shattered by making work available to a large mass of people. Instead you reinforce its connection to cult and thus ritual is re-inforced. Unlike Benjamin's beliefs, art works produced through modern technology are not necessarily oppositional to tradition, nor are they guaranteed to emancipate the masses.

Benjamin opposed the religious and ritual context for art as he wanted art works to play a political role in emancipating the masses. But his interpretation of ritual is derived from a modern Western point of view. From this standpoint, ritual belongs to the world of magic and superstition. Westerners would seek to dominate nature through science and rationality and not be concerned with the beyond. From an Eastern perspective, the performance of ritual mediates the continuum between an inner spiritual and outer material world.[10] Within these cultures, the sense of identity is derived from a metonymic view of the universe in which man is continuous with the context in which he finds himself. An example of this exists within Aboriginal cultures where the inner self extends to mythic and mystical spheres that are experienced communally. The self also projects itself into the landscape that is sacred. Metonymic thinking implies that the sacred space of the landscape and the religious belief structure are interrelated.

This mode of thinking is also present within Indian culture. For example, Uma is the Indian Goddess for creativity, power and energy and carvings of this statue portray a likeness of the Goddess. Westerners would see this statue as a symbolic representation of the Goddess. But if you use an Indian or metonymic way of thinking about it, which is what happens when the statue is worshipped, then the carving is the partial manifestation of the Goddess herself. Energy, power and creativity are perceived as interrelated within this object. So, from an Eastern perspective, the purpose of art and the role of ritual is not defined through its external characteristics. Instead it allows the viewer/worshipper to partake in the power of the object.

Just as Benjamin did not appreciate the metonymic mode and the interior energy of objects, his notion of time was linear and historical. In contrast, the Eastern notion of time is cyclical and contextual. According to Ramanujan, time has changing moods and properties. Certain hours are auspicious and others inauspicious. Units of time

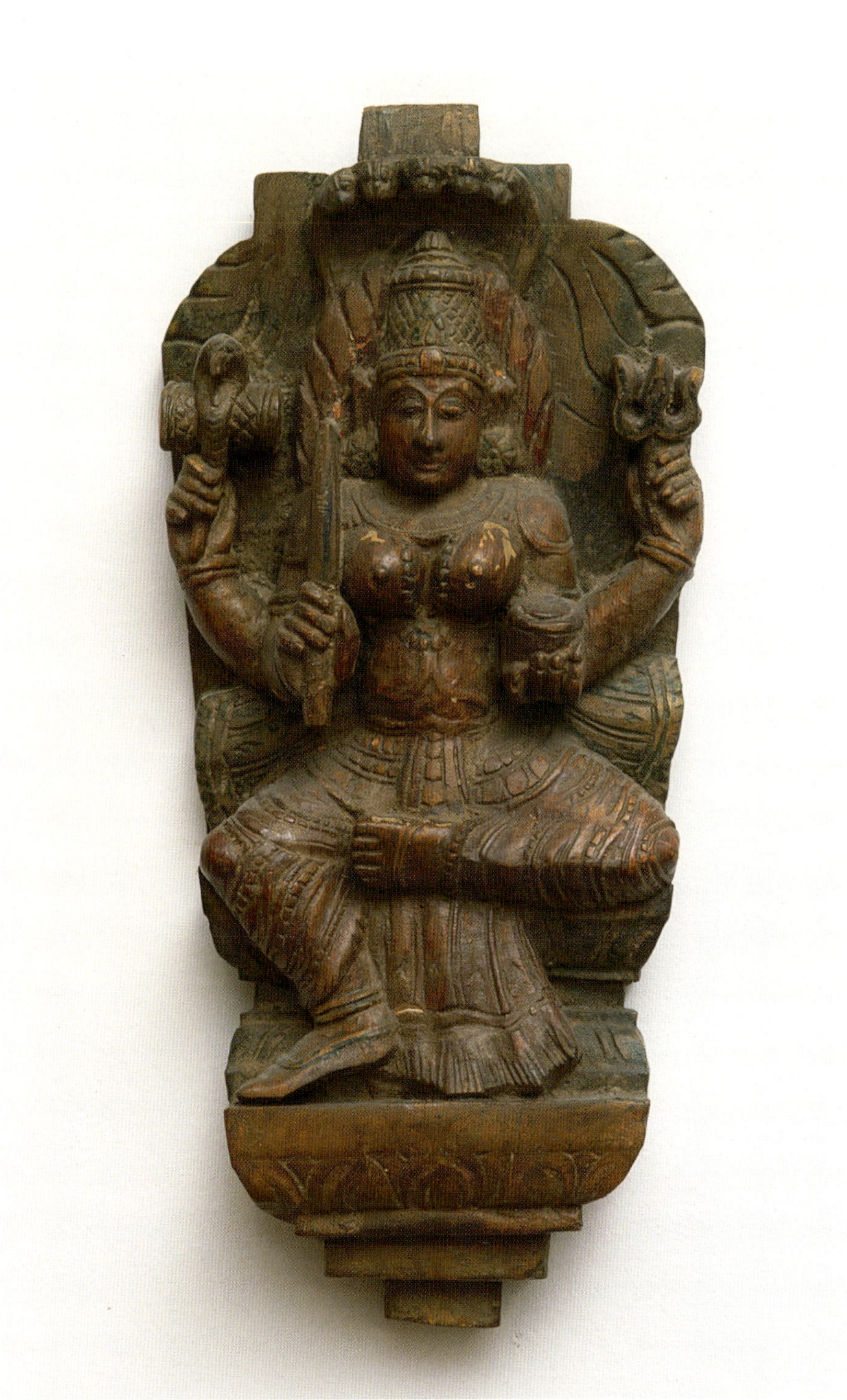

Anonymous *Uma*, 1920.
Indian wood-carving,
rosewood,
c. 29.5 x 14 cm.
Collection: Alan Roland.

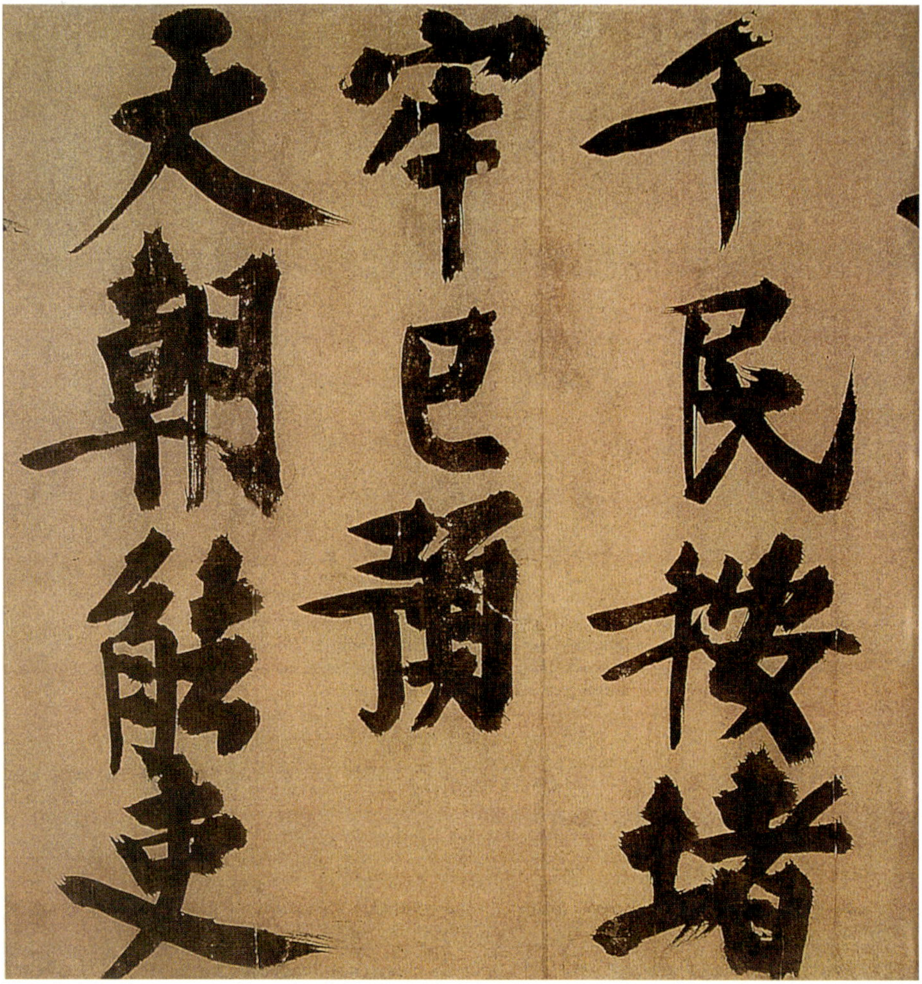

‘The energy that comes into an art work, that is known as *ch’i*, is the expression of the internal physical, emotional and spiritual state of the artist.’

Yeh-lu Ch’u-ts’ai (1190-1344) *Poem of Farewell to Liu Man*, (section 2), dated 1240. Handscroll, ink on paper, 36.5 x 284.5 cm. Collection: Metropolitan Museum of Art, New York. Bequest of John M. Crawford Jr., 1988.

breed their own kinds of melodies and cycles of time their own politics and religions. What counts is the particular rather than universal. Benjamin also failed to appreciate the importance of *ch'i* or internal energy. In China, the drawing of calligraphic characters is a spiritual discipline and is done in a meditative state. The Chinese painter seeks to capture, through calligraphic brushwork, the spirit beyond physical likeness. In describing a Chinese painting, it is necessary to refer both to the work and to the physical and spiritual condition of the painter. When the 'breath' of a painter, and thus of his work, stimulates a viewer's response, his painting projects a life and energy beyond physical representation. (*see*, Wen C. Fong, 1992, pp. 4-5; Mai-mai Sze, 1959, pp. 58-62.)

In Western terms, one can think of *ch'i* as the energy generated in art works by the hand and evidenced through nuances and imperfections. Whereas in Chinese calligraphy the quality of the line and different pressures of a stroke in drawings and prints creates another dimension that contributes to the aesthetic power of the art work. In reproductions, this extra dimension is flattened out.

Within Benjamin's framework the only art works that are valued are those that are mechanically reproduced and whose purpose is solely seen within the terms of a socio-political agenda. What Benjamin has not taken into account is how artistic vision crosses over all media, whether mechanical or non-mechanical. Within Western culture individual artists innovate to establish their own visual language and this is as true of photographers and film-makers as it is of painters. The highest value is given to work that conveys the unique vision of an artist. Yet in all media there are a limited number of artists who are capable of expressing an artistic vision. Often the greater the level of artistic vision, the smaller the audience that the art work attracts. Few people in Sweden saw Ingmar Bergman's films and in India films by Satyajit Ray had a very limited audience.

In conclusion, Benjamin's critique, in the context of greater knowledge of Asian cultures and aesthetics, is no longer accurate or applicable today. The huge waves of Asian immigration to the United States and Australia starting in the mid-sixties, and the development of a global economy, heralded the opening of a global horizon. What I am proposing is that it is now possible to develop a conceptual framework that incorporates Eastern aesthetic and cognitive modes. This framework outlines how the artistic process mediates the continuum between the inner world of the artist and its outer manifestation in the art work. Whether it is achieved via a mechanized tool like a scanner, xerox, film or computer, or by a paintbrush, there is an endless passing from inner to outer. This argument is missing from Benjamin's critique and is why his ideas are too limited for the art world of our time.

Notes

1 Irving Sandler states that: '... in the 1980s photography was promoted as the exemplary post modern art. The major proponent of photography and postmodern art theory was Rosalind Krauss, one of the founders of the art journal, *October*. Krauss decreed that painting was outworn and had to be jettisoned. She and her co-editor, Annette Michelson, declared that it had been '. . . consigned to deserved oblivion in the sixties'. Painting was *October*'s bete noire because it epitomized originality, subjectivity, uniqueness and authenticity. Moreover, it was esoteric, elitist, and appealed to bourgeois appetites ...'. Theorist Craig Owens asserted that as a means of production painting was technologically 'academic' and 'moribund' and attempts to revive it were futile. Irving Sandler, *A Sweeper-Up After Artists. A Memoir*, Thames & Hudson, 2003, pp. 316-318.

2 Walter Benjamin, 'The work of Art in the Age of Mechanical Reproduction', *Illuminations*, Harcourt Brace & World, New York, 1968.

3 Benjamin gives the example of Atget's photos of deserted Paris streets, which he says 'acquire a hidden political significance ... . They demand a specific kind of approach; free-floating contemplation is not appropriate to them. They stir the viewer; he feels challenged by them in a new way'. Ibid., p. 226.

4 Benjamin states, '. . . the instant the criterion of authenticity ceases to be applicable to artistic production, the total function of art is reversed. Instead of being based on ritual, it begins to be based on another practice – politics'. Ibid., p. 224.

5 Marcel Eliade, *The Sacred and the Profane*, Harcourt Brace, New York, 1959.

6 As Richard Vine has pointed out, while Benjamin's process was dialectical, his recorded thought is more like a string, not even a sequence, of alleged 'aperçus'.

7 See page 19 for an illustration of metonymic thinking. For an illustration of the Kathakali dancers see pages 75 and 76.

8 Milton Singer, *When a great tradition modernizes: An anthropological approach to Indian civilization*, Praeger, New York, 1972.

9 A.K. Ramanujan, 'Is there an Indian Way of Thinking? An Informal Essay', included in *India through Hindu Categories*, edited by McKim Marriott, Sage Publications, 1980.

10 Alan Roland, *In Search of Self in India and Japan: Towards a Cross-Cultural Psychology*, Princeton University Press, 1988.

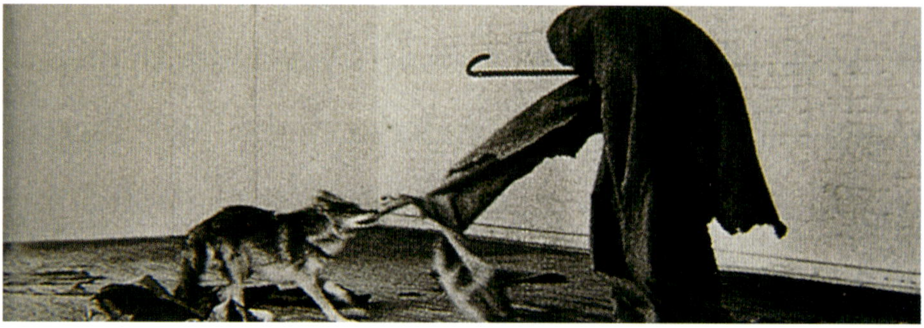

Chapter **3**

The Impact of Joseph Beuys

In the late 1960s, when I started painting in New York City, artists for the most part made no reference in their work to objects. For two decades the work seen in galleries and museums was non-representational. It was at this period that I discovered Joseph Beuys's works on paper and attended his performances. His performance actions incorporated everyday objects with which he felt a strong personal connection. This was also true of his use of such mundane materials as fat and felt. I was especially struck by the fact that his drawings contained references to objects and I still have present in my mind his depictions of whales, boats, sleds, animals and vases. This exposure to his art triggered a new development in my work. I started making ink drawings and among the images I used were a bird, ship, tunnel, house, trap, trapdoor, window, leaf and table. I associated these images with transition, obstacles, growth, security, flight and isolation.

Joseph Beuys, *Coyote. I Like America and America Likes Me*, 1974. Photograph: Caroline Tisdale. © V. G. Bild-Kunst, Bonn. © Joseph Beuys Licensed by VISCOPY, Australia, 2005.

Unlike Beuys, who used actual objects in his sculptures and performances, in my work I was concerned to convey the archetypal presence of an image. I did this by combining the following steps. In both the drawings and the paintings the scale of the image was small. Firstly, I disassociated the object from its habitual surroundings. I also excluded all detail and anecdote. In this way the image avoided becoming descriptive but became more of an archetype, invested with personal meanings. In composing the drawings I placed the image in the middle of a sheet of paper, then I worked with ink, using layers of cross-hatching to provide a context for the image. But it was the large white space surrounding the drawn image that played a crucial role in helping to elevate the image into an archetype.

Another influence in my work at that time was my discovery of the Etruscan civilization when I visited Tarquinia and the Villa Guilia in Rome. I felt drawn to the beauty of the culture's remaining objects – the urns, amphoras and vessels. It was especially the colour of the vessels, earthen and veering to *terra rosa*, that appealed to me. I also loved their shapes, some large at the top and narrowing down, others swelling in the middle to mould an almost pure circle. They had long necks and long stems, sometimes diamond-shaped, wide at the center before descending to a point.

But there was another reason why these objects struck such a deep chord in me. The vessels evoked the awareness of another realm. They had a transcendent quality, allowing me to feel in touch with the unknown, a realm of the invisible.

Today I have a better understanding of that response because of my knowledge of Aboriginal art. Traditional Aboriginal artists also bring another reality into being. Within their culture there is a mythic orientation to the landscape, and artists who are

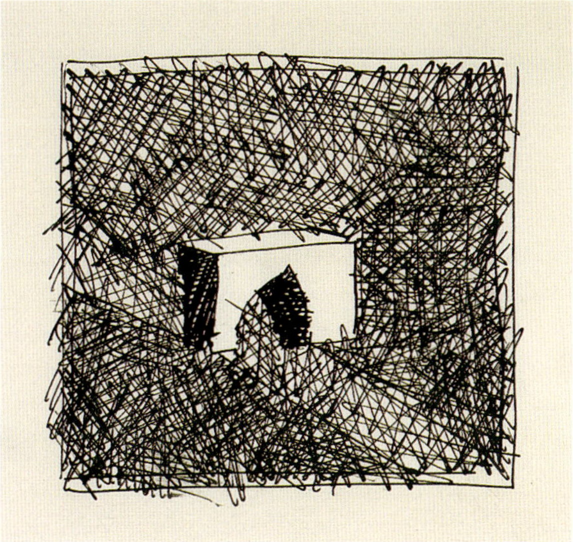

Denise Green, *Arch*, 1976. Ink on paper, 35 x 35 cm. Courtesy Anthony Grant Inc., New York. Photograph: Nicholas Walster.

custodians of sacred sites paint directly on the rock face, or on their own bodies, or on tree bark to bring into being the presence of another realm. When the Aboriginal artist marks a circle on a rock, to Western eyes it may look like the incised depiction of a face. But to the Aboriginal people it is not simply a representation or picture of the ancestral being, it is the very presence of the being itself.

What is involved here is a process of metonymic thinking which implies the fusion of an inner spiritual and outer material world. When the Aboriginal artist externalizes his or her state of mind on the rock face, instead of being the image of an invisible entity the ancestral figure becomes part of the real world.

Aboriginal artists relate to the land on two different levels which combine their day to day reality, and at the same time a reality permeated by a transcendent quality of their myths and what they mean to the people.

For me the Etruscan objects also function on two different levels. The vessels are concrete and mundane objects, yet they have a transcendent quality that evokes the spirit of another age. I find that what I share with Beuys is a resonance with traditional cultures: for me it is a connection with Asian and Aboriginal cultures, for Beuys an

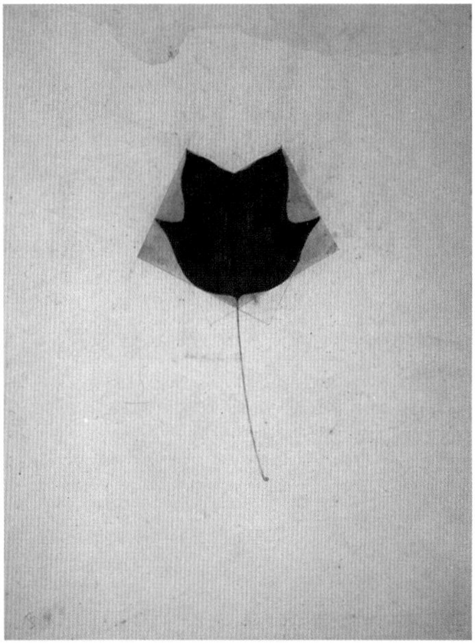

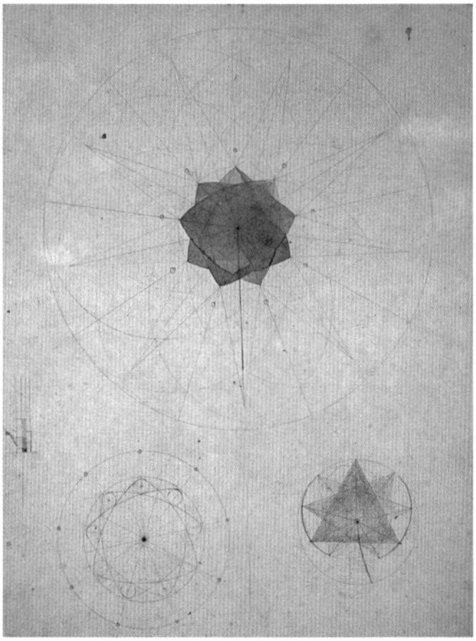

Left:
Joseph Beuys, *Tulipidendrin Lyrofolium*, 1948. 35 x 24.8 cm. Collection: Erich Marx, Hamburger Bahnhof Museum, Berlin. © Joseph Beuys Licensed by VISCOPY, Australia, 2005.

Right:
Joseph Beuys, *Lady's Cloak*, 1948. 33.5 x 24.8 cm. Collection: Erich Marx, Hamburger Bahnhof Museum, Berlin. © Joseph Beuys Licensed by VISCOPY, Australia, 2005.

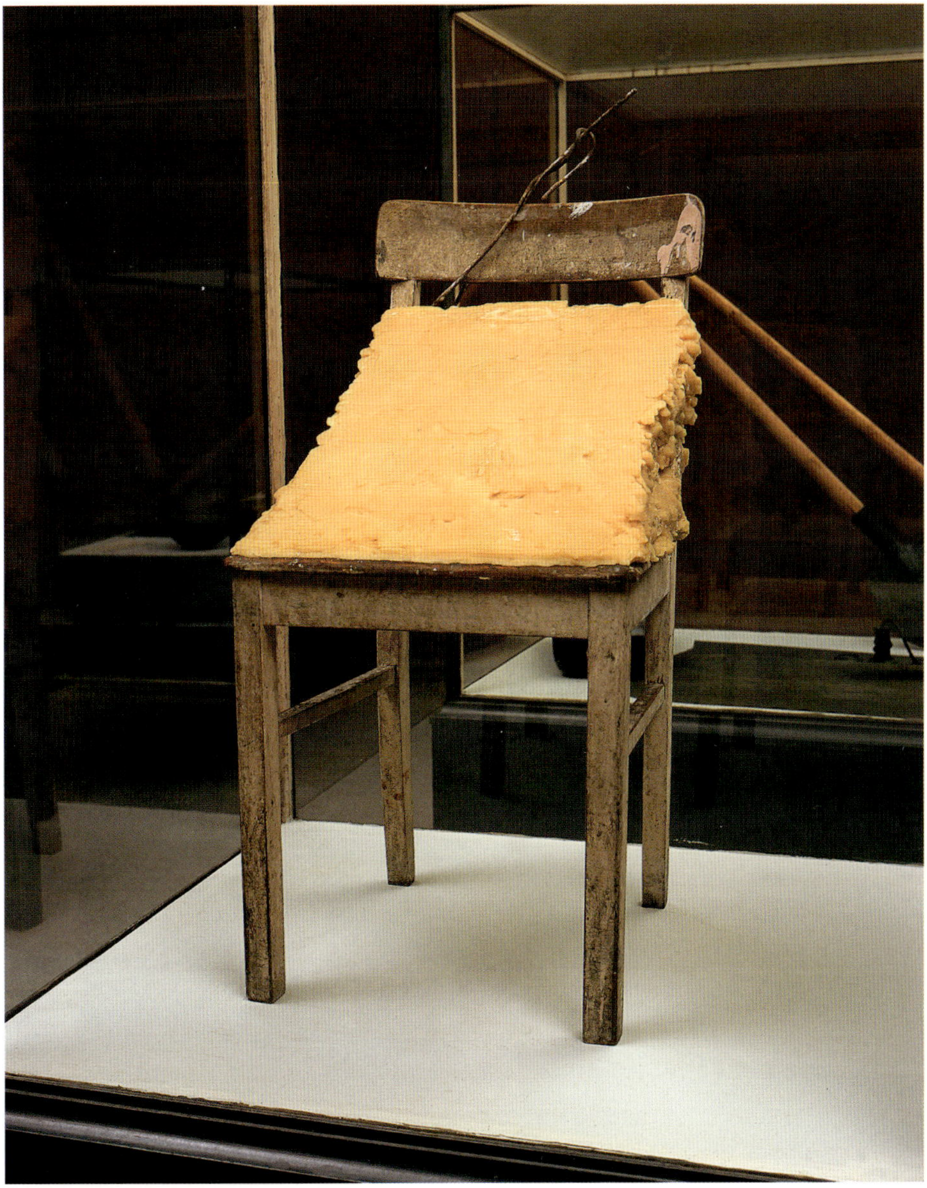

Joseph Beuys, *Stuhl mit Fett*, 1963. Wooden chair with fat, 94.5 x 41.6 x 47.5 cm. Stoher Collection, Hessisches Landesmuseum, Darmstadt. Photograph: Wolfgang Fuhrmannek. © V G Bild-Kunst, Bonn.

intense interest in Nordic and Germanic mythology and his knowledge of Central Asian societies.

Beuys is interested in the healing and transforming properties of the materials he uses in his sculptures. The origin of Beuys's involvement with fat and felt can be traced back to 1945 when he had an encounter with the Tartars who rescued him from an air crash. 'They covered my body in fat to help it regenerate warmth, and wrapped it in felt as an insulator to keep it warm', Beuys recounts.[1] These substances had healing properties that helped overcome the trauma, and Beuys adopted fat and felt in his sculptures to suggest the passage from one state of being to another.

From a normal Western perspective, materials such as felt and fat are substances known for their physical properties, but from an anthroposophical perspective these substances can also have subtle non-physical properties transcending their concrete nature and taking on other meanings. For example, in Beuys's sculpture, *Fat Chair*, he combined a chair with a large wedge of fat. Beuys said the right-angled corner of the chair symbolized for him the mechanistic tendency of the human mind, while the fat was a metaphor for spirituality and change. In making the sculpture he placed the fat on top of the chair so that the fat and its properties are dominant.

Beuys also uses images of swans, hares and stags. This is a return to the imagery with which he felt an intuitive connection when as a child he heard stories of Nordic mythology. For Beuys, animals came to possess special powers and to embody a connection with the beyond.[2] In his drawings of shepherds and ironmongers, he rendered them as shamans communicating with another realm.[3] Beuys identified with the shaman and wanted to provoke a transformation of society through art.[4]

As to the evolution of my own work, in 1988 I re-introduced the vessel shape in my paintings and they became part of my forms of reference. In 2001 another new turn could be identified in a group of paintings called *Surveillance* when I started using the vessel shapes to convey a metonymic way of thinking. Writing about these works in *Art & Australia*, Laura Murray Cree reported that *Surveillance 1, 2* and *3,* '...were painted during another period of intense emotion. Green and several other New York artists were threatened with eviction from their loft studios through the action of ruthless developers. Overlapping forms in the works signify the impinging of public and private spheres'.[5] In my case the surveillance involved hidden cameras focused day and night on every coming and going from my studio. The discovery of this invasion of my private space evoked a state of mind which was transferred directly into my painting. For me everything had become permeable. Instead of object and space being stable, as in other paintings like *Azzuro di Cobalto Puro,* now object and space were interpenetrated.

Though still drawn to the aesthetic of modern Western painting, I find that for me a strong affinity persists with the work of Beuys and with Aboriginal art. What we possibly share is a process whereby, through art, we gain access to a state of mind that communicates metonymically. Image and media become substances of transformation, allowing us to express an invisible spirituality.

Notes

1 Caroline Tisdale, *Joseph Beuys*, The Solomon R. Guggenheim Museum, New York, 1979.

2 Ibid.

3 Anne Seymour, *Joseph Beuys: Drawings*, Victoria and Albert Museum, London, 1983.

4 Tisdale, op. cit.

5 Laura Murray Cree. 'Resonating: Denise Green. A synergy of form and feeling', *Art & Australia*, Sydney, vol. 39, December 2001, pp.224-226.

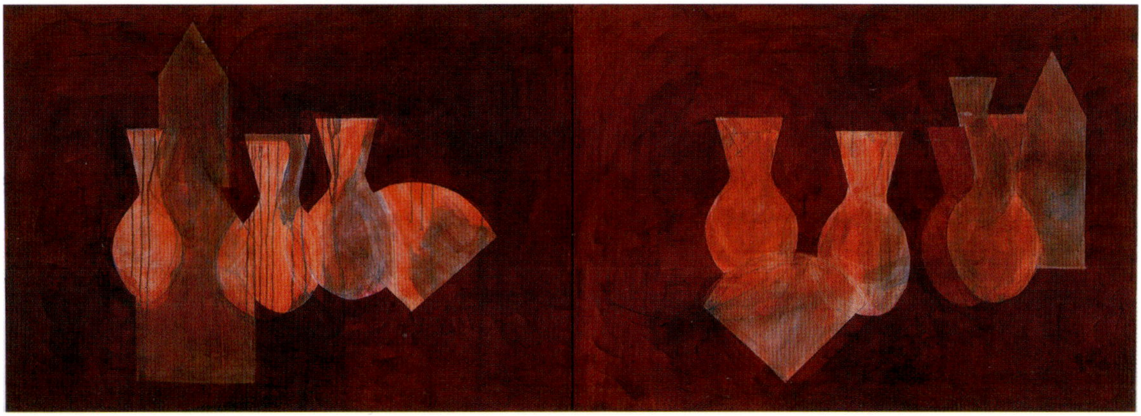

Denise Green, *Surveillance # 2*, 2001. Acrylic on canvas, 112 x 316 cm. Courtesy Christine Abrahams Gallery, Melbourne. Photograph: Nicholas Walster.

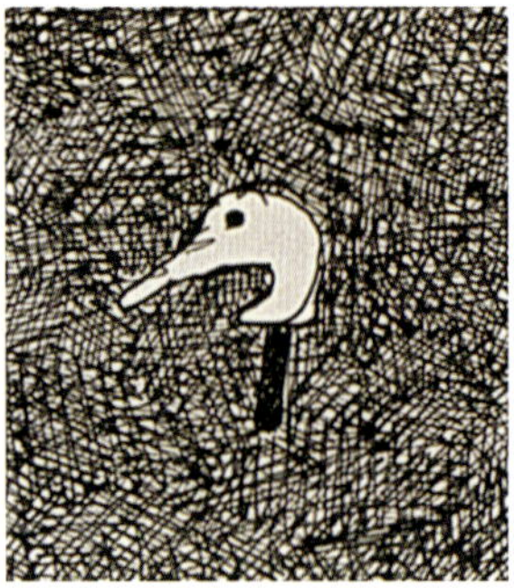

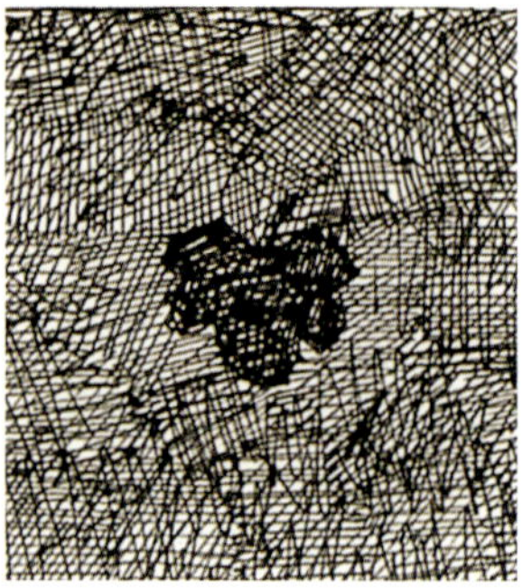

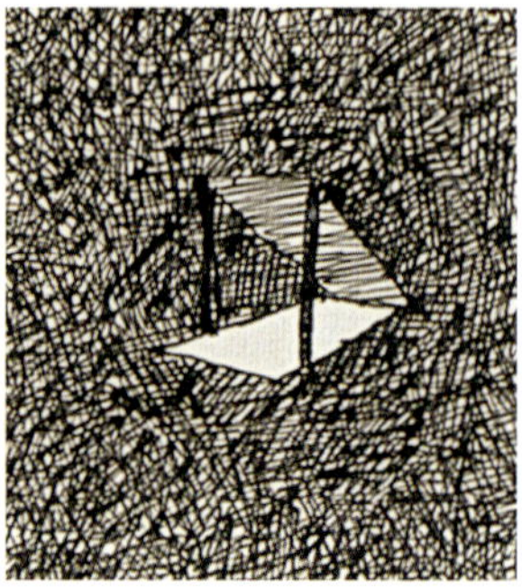

Chapter **4**

Away from Australia: My Aesthetic in the 1970s

Left:
Denise Green, *Decoy*, 1976. Ink on paper, 35 x 35 cm. Courtesy Annandale Galleries, Sydney. Photograph: Nicholas Walster.

Centre:
Denise Green, *Leaf*, 1976. Ink on paper, 35 x 35 cm. Collection: Museum of Modern Art, New York. Photograph: Nicholas Walster.

Right:
Denise Green, *Trapdoor*, 1976. Ink on paper 35 x 35 cm. Courtesy Galerie Asbaek, Copenhagen. Photograph: Nicholas Walster.

Artistic identity is formed as much by what you admire as what you reject. After four years in Paris, I arrived in New York in 1969. Artists from all parts of the world were drawn to New York, then the center of the art world. It was such a large city, but once they arrived they found that the art world was a small community. What was helpful for me was the opportunity of re-inventing myself through the encounter with different ideas, some of which I greatly admired and others that I shunned. In this way I was forced to develop another kind of perspective on my experience. I connected with the energy of the city and loved the easy access I had to three generations of major artists. The older generation I met in classrooms, the middle generation by hanging out in bars, and the younger artists were contacted through chance encounters on the street, or in diners in Soho and Tribeca.

My work was still at a formative stage and it was to develop in a number of different contexts. These included the artistic and intellectual worlds introduced to me by my former husband, Bruce Wolmer, and my studies in the graduate program at Hunter College. Other contexts included my association with radical intellectual groups centered around *Telos* and *Semiotext(e)* magazines, my collaboration with feminist enterprises such as *Heresies* magazine, and my meetings with artists in the Soho/Tribeca neighborhood where I lived. There was also the pressure to win recognition from galleries and museums.

Bruce Wolmer was a poet, art critic and intellectual who knew many people in the art world. He had worked briefly at the Museum of Modern Art and with Praeger Publishers and was perceptive about the newest intellectual trends that were to move from a marginal place into mainstream culture. In the early seventies he returned to graduate school at John Hopkins University where Jacques Derrida, François Lyotard and Michel Foucault were lecturing in one of the first programs on French theoretical discourse. Among the many artists I met through him were Scott Burton and Joel Shapiro, and the poets John Ashbery, Ted Greenwald and Ann Lauterbach. We had endless discussions about art, and I recognized that a battle was taking place between painters and conceptual artists. Through our network of friends I learned about the graduate program at Hunter College and enrolled so that I could be part of the dialogue taking place there. Ralph Humphrey, Tony Smith, Doug Ohlson and Robert Morris were on the fine arts faculty and in the art history department were Gene Goosen, Rosalind Krauss and Leo Steinberg. After I enrolled I heard that Rothko had been invited to teach for a year and that Motherwell was giving seminars.

Shortly after my arrival in New York I saw a major body of Rothko's work on exhibit at the Metropolitan Museum. The discovery of these works inspired me. But it was even more than that. I felt spellbound and captivated. Here I had encountered the transformation of materials into pure feelings and evidence of a state of mind that commanded my respect and evoked a deep response in me. Seeing a large number of his works transported me to another plane.

In the classroom Rothko was often a silent and brooding presence. He did not invite a warm exchange with the students. Many were art history majors who questioned art's function and challenged him about the viability of easel painting. Rothko remained aloof and quiet, never engaging intellectually with these ideas. What I remember most is how he hovered there, watching us debate about aesthetic theory. His withdrawal and lack of energy may have been related to poor health, but his silence seemed to be an unwillingness to engage with those who opposed painting. Yet the fact of his presence every week in that classroom reinforced my conviction about the validity of painting at a time when it was under attack by the avant-garde.

Other faculty members, like Ralph Humphrey and Tony Smith, were easily in tune with the aesthetic sensibilities of their students, helping them to develop their own personal ways of working. There was a lot or theorizing in the art world at that time and in the classroom Robert Morris and Robert Barry argued against painting, stating that its cultural meanings were exhausted. They promoted the major intellectual and critical attitudes to which the Conceptual and Earth Art movements belonged. In his work, Morris had redefined the limits of sculpture by taking it out of the gallery and into the world. He discussed the increasing dematerialization of the art object and his articles were appearing in *Art Forum*. But Morris was a very destructive force for many of us who wanted to develop as painters. He conveyed the idea that to prevail in the art world and gain historical relevance, artists had to proceed by pursuing the agenda of the avant-garde by pushing art one step further. He seemed to infer that we would automatically fail if we worked with the medium of paint in his class. Because of this, the interaction and dialogue between those of us who were in his class became important. As a way of fighting back and asserting our identity as painters, several of us started writing and publishing essays about art. For a year and a half I wrote a monthly column for a major art magazine, including a review of Morris's show at the

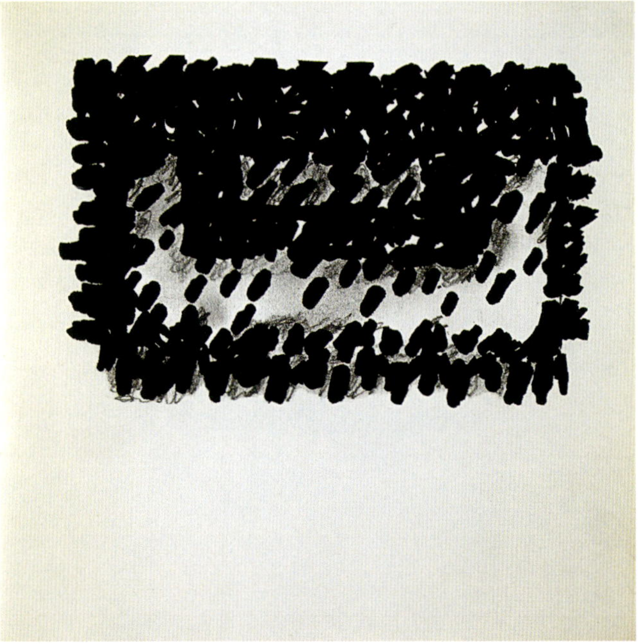

Ralph Humphrey, *Studies*, 1977. Photograph from book of that title, offset lithography, 15 x 15 cm. Courtesy of Amy Baker Sandback.

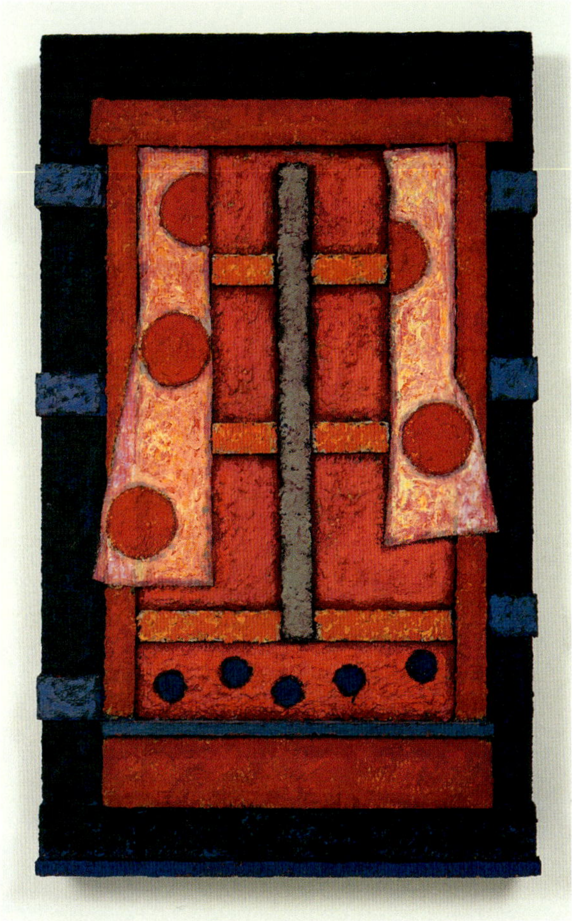

Leo Castelli Gallery in which I critiqued his point of view. But there were other students who were so influenced by Morris's views that they simply gave up painting.

I feel that modernist art has become a tradition that is passed down from the presence and words of one generation of artists to another. Rothko said that his generation had taken abstraction as far as it could go and there would be a return to some kind of figurative imagery in painting. He referred to Milton Avery's work. From this I carried away some kind of license that allowed me to return to the use of a reference in my paintings. I also gained a sense of painting's continuity, and the way

Ralph Humphrey, *Thin Edge*, 1981-82. Acrylic and modelling paste on canvas and wood, 156 x 91 x 62 cm. Private collection. Courtesy Daniel Weinberg Gallery, Los Angeles.

my generation could reinvigorate it through the use of archetypal images. From Rothko, I also absorbed an influence that was not conveyed through words. Motherwell said that Rothko could act like a shaman. I felt he could access an inner realm and externalize it in his work through the use of colour and light spread over the entire surface. Painting actualized the essence of his internal world. The essentials of his approach stayed in my mind and I held onto them as I developed my own aesthetic.

I did my thesis, a study of Rothko, with Ralph Humphrey – another artist on the faculty at Hunter College. While Rothko was a powerful and inspired presence, with Humphrey one could engage in close dialogue. My exchange with him pollinated my work. He was a passionate mediator in attempts to integrate my responses to Rothko's work into my own. In his own work he was a proto-Minimalist, responding to Rothko's aesthetic, but taking it somewhere else. He deepened his stretchers by four or five inches and built up the surface with myriad touches of thickened paint. Rothko's work was about pure light conveyed through thin washes of colour, while Humphrey weighted the paint so that it became opaque. Thereby, he emphasized the materiality of the surface, and the objectness of the painting.

During those years of looking for work and artists, apart from Ralph Humphrey,

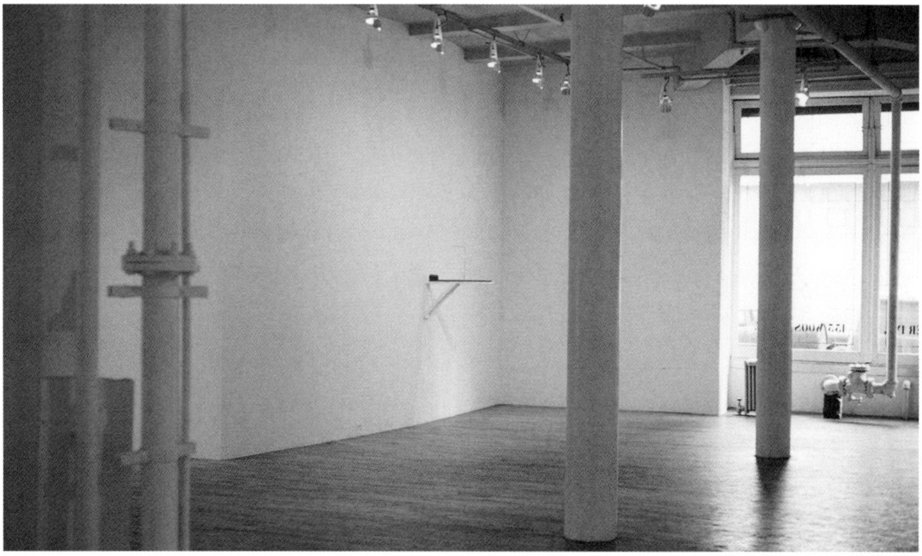

Joel Shapiro, Installation view, Paula Cooper Gallery, New York, 1974. © Joel Shapiro/Artists' Rights Society (ARS), New York.

whose aesthetic attracted me, the important figures included such painters as James Bishop, Joe Zucker and Neil Jenney and the sculptors Scott Burton and Donald Judd. The works of Jennifer Bartlett and Susan Rothenberg also acted as a stimulant.

But it was Joel Shapiro's work that had a profound influence on me, specially his breakthrough between 1972 and 1975 when he made small-size carvings of a boat, a coffin, a bridge, or cast a tiny house and small chair in iron. These objects were so connected to his state of mind that they became metonyms that spoke of his life. I could feel the energy in that work. He talked about registering his mood, and claimed that each piece represented a different kind of feeling. I didn't realize at the time that this was my process too. Perhaps that is why his words were so important. He spoke for my own way of working.

There was something vulnerable and approachable about Joel during those years. Indecisiveness was a part of it, and self-doubt. It came as a shock to hear him say that the 'I' was the subject of his work. What did this mean? In spite of his self-doubt, how intriguing that Joel would have the confidence and security to use his own experiences – that he was open and direct enough to employ the happenings in his life. He referred to his two years in the Peace Corps in India. I wondered if the

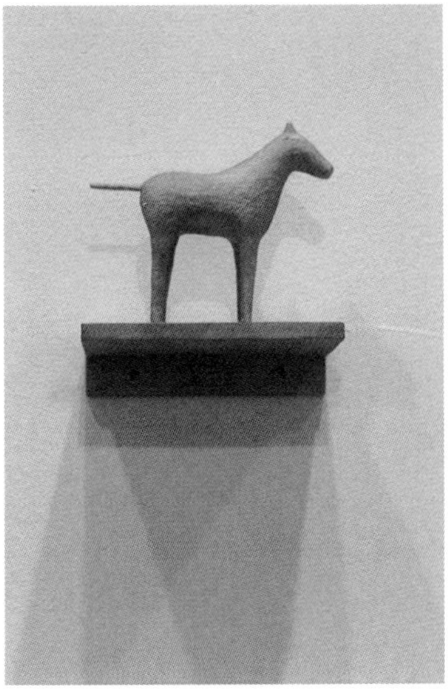

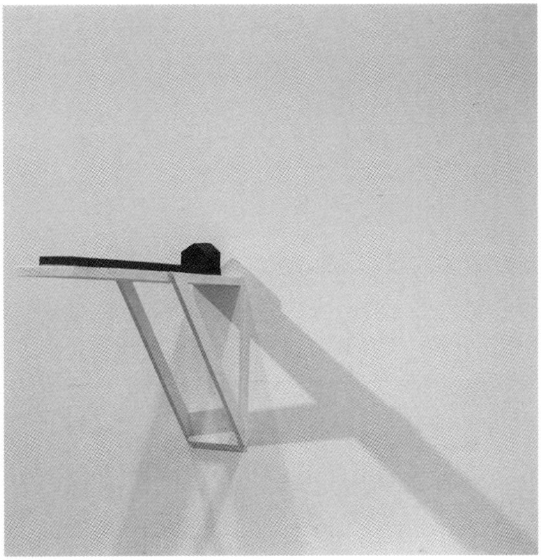

Left:
Joel Shapiro, *Untitled*, 1973-74. Bronze, 1 of 3, 12.1 x 13.5 x 8.3 cm. Collection: Carol Selle. © Joel Shapiro/Artists' Rights Society (ARS), New York.

Right:
Joel Shapiro, *Untitled*, 1974-76. Bronze with wood base, 1 of 3, 7.5 x 68 x 6.7 cm. © Joel Shapiro/Artists' Rights Society (ARS), New York.

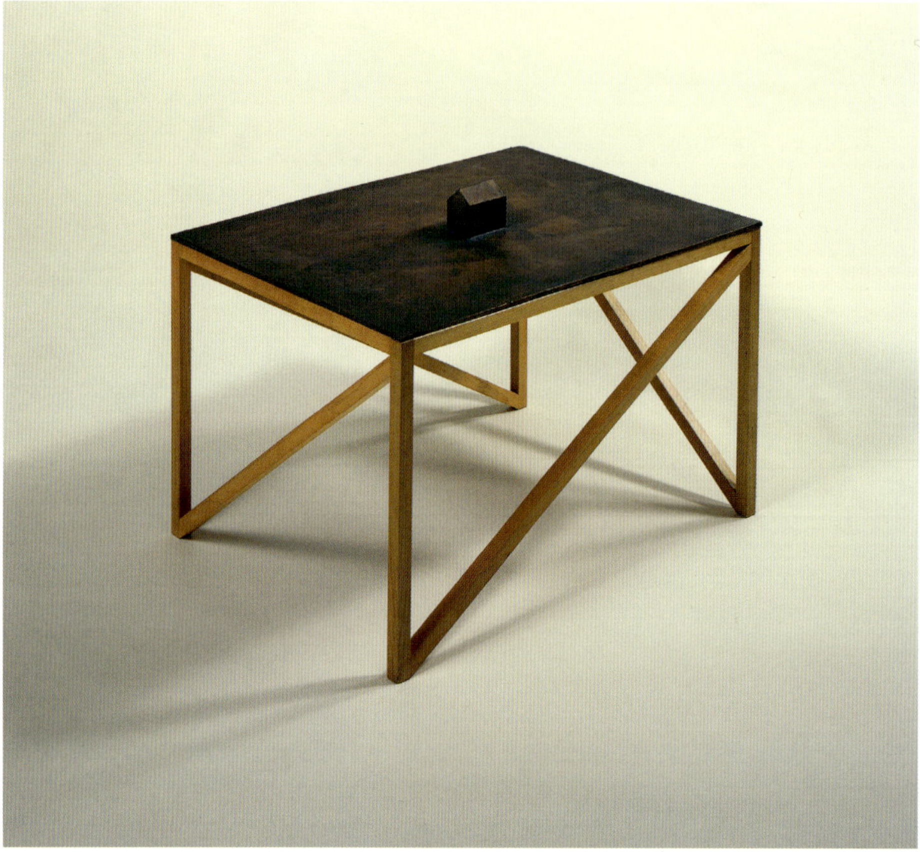

Joel Shapiro, ***Untitled* (House on Field), 1975-76. Bronze on wood base, 1 of 2. Collection: Whitney Museum of American Art, New York. Photograph © 1997: Whitney Museum of American Art, New York. Photograph: Jerry L. Thompson.**

introduction of the horse and bird shapes owed something to this experience. And there was also the sense of impotence about the possibility of making art at all. His shapes and their autobiographical references resounded with such implications.

Joel's words empowered me. They were charged with electricity. Just reading my notes from those years reminds me how curious I was about what he meant. Some of his comments referred to setting up an archetype instead of subject matter. In the boat shapes, for example, he did not intend to illustrate an object. Simplified, refined and devoid of detail, the image could be elevated into an archetype. He said that the horse piece was about 'horseness' in all its tenses rather than the illustration of a horse at a specific time or place. He also said there was no specific source for this image, that it was a manifestation of his state of mind. It is what it is – an archetype, but also a manifestation. This attitude is metonymic. When you manifest your state of mind through the process of painting or sculpting, it becomes an embodiment of it.

At this time the images in my work functioned in two ways simultaneously. They were both an archetype and a reflection of state of mind. I was making ink drawings and searching for shapes which had a personal meaning. The images I introduced into the paintings were, among others, a window, trapdoor, vessel, chair, tunnel, and house. Each shape was depicted in one colour, as a single, centralized object.

I realized that when objects are drawn from one's interior world for translation into a painting, they lose their reference to specific objects in the external world. Instead, they enter the imagination as archetypal images. Once translated into paint they re-materialize as fictive objects incorporating both the self and object. These objects may be seen as inert and abstract, yet they activate desire and memory, and call up feelings and emotions like longing, fears, hopes, expectations and disappointments. I was interested in creating this fictional consciousness by elevating the images into archetypes and I conveyed the archetypal presence in several different ways. In both drawings and paintings the scale of the image was small, so that the fictive object was placed in the middle of the canvas or sheet of paper. In the drawings, I worked with ink, using layers of crosshatching to provide a context for the image. The white space of the page surrounding the drawing helped convey its archetypal presence. In the paintings, I created layers of paint ridged by the palette knife to establish a context for the image. Both the colour and the layered field created by the palette knife contributed to the archetypal qualities of the image.

For instance, after the break up with my husband and my move to another studio I began a painting of a house image. He had decided to go to Graduate School in Baltimore and asked that I join him full time and give up my studio and my life as an artist in New York City. At this time my work had begun to be recognized through a show at the Whitney Museum Art Resources Center and I decided to devote myself to painting and maintain my identity as an artist in New York. I now realize that the house shape I painted then was an aerial view of the six story loft building on Broome Street in Soho where Bruce and I had lived. Soho, which is now a tourist mecca, was then a community of serious, often impoverished artists. Our place on Broome Street was also my studio. It was identified with my ambition to be a painter, to be part

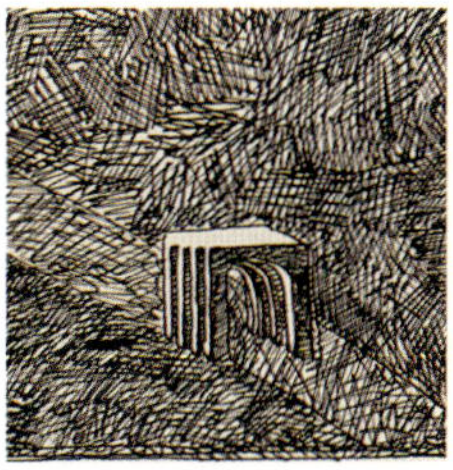

Denise Green, *Gateway*, 1976. Ink on paper, 25 x 27 cm. Collection Museum of Modern Art, New York. Photograph: Nicholas Walster.

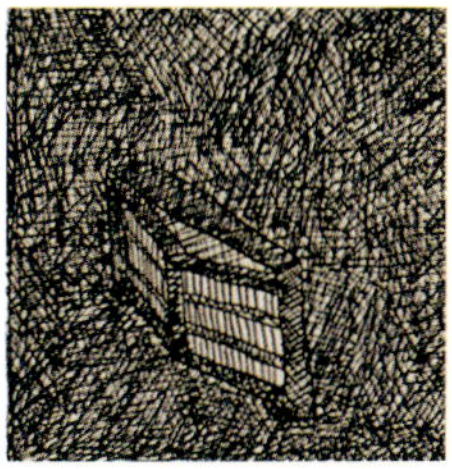

Denise Green, *Tower Gate*, 1976. Ink on paper, 24 x 25 cm. Collection: Museum of Modern Art, New York. Photograph: Nicholas Walster.

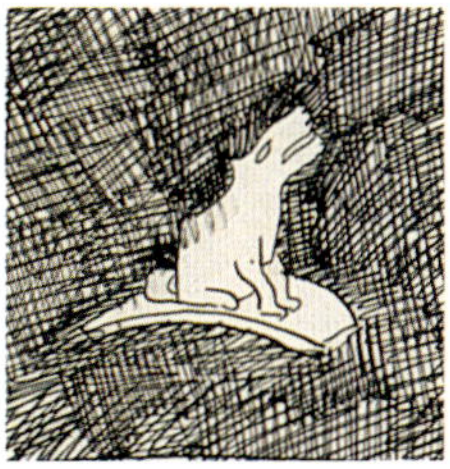

Denise Green, *Hybrid Animal*, 1976. Ink on paper, 35 x 35 cm. Courtesy Galerie Heike Curtze, Vienna. Photograph: Nicholas Walster.

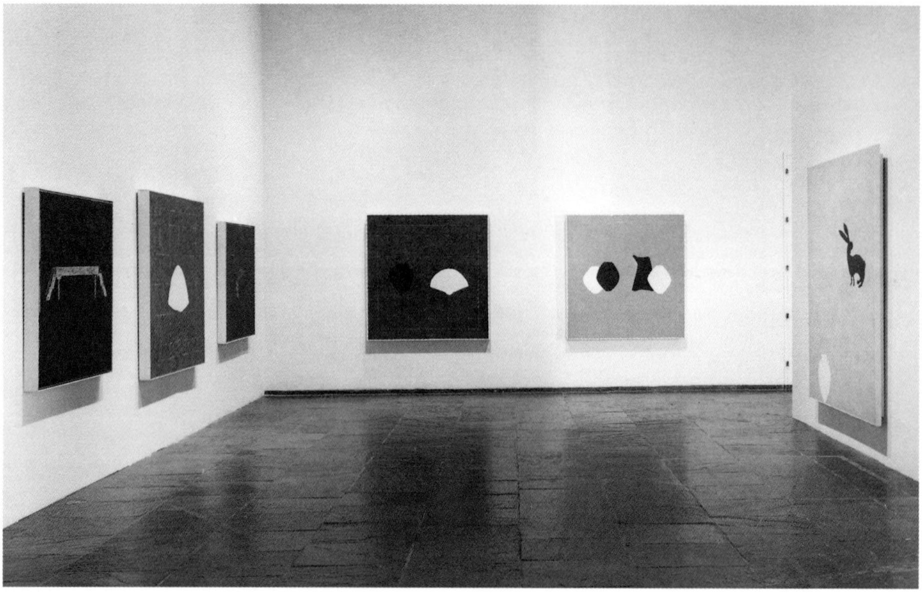

Installation View. Denise Green in ***New Image Painting***, exhibition, 5 December-20 January, 1979. Whitney Museum of American Art, New York. Photograph © Whitney Museum of American Art, New York. Photograph: Geoffrey Clements.

of the art world in New York, and taken seriously as an artist.

A sensitive friend described the house shape as an isolated, mysterious, haunting image. She also saw it as a quiet and lonely image, but a warm one – an image of a space, a structure, a dwelling, and perhaps a symbol that captured the life of an artist with an inward focus. She also saw it as the ghost of a house, glowing with an interior light.

This became a time of determination, of being alone in the world and directing all my energies into painting. A feeling of sadness took over because the life with Bruce no longer existed. Yet the building in which we had lived together had also been my workspace. It was symbolic of the small-scale buildings of Soho where I felt I belonged as an artist amidst a community of artists. I, as an artist, was identified with this house image. It was a powerful representation of a space where I expressed my state of mind and where I existed as a painter. It was a space I could never give up.

Another important influence during this period was the work of Joseph Beuys with whom I shared the sense of a personal connection to the image and the development of what I later termed the metonymic process. The use of images, both personal and abstract, was derived from conversations with Joel and the experience of his work. Looking back, I realize he was working metonymically because his pieces were a reflection of his inner world. But even more importantly, my interaction with him gave me permission to include the 'I' in my work.

Artistic identity is not fixed. It can be deeply affected by the cultural, intellectual and aesthetic attitudes of a particular time. The 1970s was a period of tremendous turmoil and ferment among radical artistic and intellectual groups. Deeply involved and thus affected, I lost my innocence about what it is to be an artist, and discovered

Denise Green, *House*, 1976. Oil on canvas, 122 x 122 cm. Collection: Phyllis Weil, New York. Photograph: Nicholas Walster.

that art is created within a social and political context. In retrospect, some of the thinking affected me in a negative way. I took a detour and then gradually resisted the intellectual attitudes toward art found among the more radical groups to which I belonged and also among conceptual artists of the time.

My association with these groups had begun in Paris during the student uprisings of May 1968. I experienced the violence of the special riot control police in the early days of the unrest. Workers and students clashed with police when demonstrating their revolt against the traditional values of consumer society, conformity and the social order. It was a moment which challenged 'institutions and knowledge, a moment of endless discussions, occupied campuses and workplaces, spontaneity and immediacy. A battle of street stones and burning cars.'[1]

This led to a sudden political awareness. I collaborated in the making of political posters at the Ecole des Beaux Arts and became interested in the Utopian thinking of Herbert Marcuse. This political interest continued after the move to New York where I became involved with radical and political artistic thinking. The critical theory of the Frankfurt School formed a strong part of the cultural milieu. Members of this school of thought argued that art should function as a critique of culture and that artists should channel a critical message to the masses. I was aware of the work and strategies of post-studio and conceptual artists who reached beyond painting, opting for film, video or performance. Evenings were spent at openings and in studios, listening to conceptual artists argue that the concept is more important than the making of an art object. They were dismissive of anyone who painted. Encounters with these conceptual artists inevitably produced a conflict within myself, yet I resisted their ideas and continued to paint.

As a natural continuation of this involvement with protest actions, from 1975 I regularly attended meetings organized by a collective called Artists Meeting for Cultural Change (AMCC). Drawn into more intellectually sophisticated forms of protest by artists within this collective who began publishing journals as a more effective strategy for cultural criticism, I subsequently worked as an editor of the feminist journal *Heresies* and also joined the editorial board of *Semiotext(e)*, a radical journal and one of the most significant publications of the time. It introduced French theory, especially the ideas of Gilles Deleuze, Felix Guattari, Jean-François Lyotard and Michel Foucault to academia and to the New York art world. Many of the ideas from May 1968 had resurfaced in the context of this group of thinkers. May 1968 had been a key political-intellectual landmark because of the students' revolt against intellectual authorities in both the University and Government. As a result of their actions, philosophers and post-Structuralists envisaged politics as needing to go beyond notions of representation and meaning. In writing, as well as the other arts, the authority of the author was under attack. Subjectivity was seen as obsolete, even reactionary. Writing was not the expression of a unique vision or belief, instead, philosophers such as Deleuze thought it should be an open, almost involuntary response to the events of one's time. I became influenced by all of this.

The attitudes and the philosophy of *Semiotext(e)* made a profound impression on my aesthetic and on my work. What was so unique in my work, the archetypal images related to the 'I', were abandoned. According to French theory, any representation related to the self through an image was to be avoided. However, my *New Image* works were vulnerable and fragile statements. They were full of feelings. They were connected to an inner state. Here I could resonate with Rothko who spoke of how paintings can be damaged by being viewed by people who are not sensitive to the artist's sensibility.

What influenced me most in *Semiotext(e)* were the theories of Deleuze and Guattari. They elaborated a conception of desire where it flowed freely and proliferated rhizomatically. I became fascinated with the rhizomatic model where, in contrast to traditional thought in which writing has a center from which ideas develop in a distinct and orderly direction, rhizomatics sprawl, making random and de-centered connections through a free flow of desire. Rhizomes expand without constraint or direction and act a-historically through forgetfulness and evasion. They are principally concerned with movement and activity. A rhizomatic painting has no meaning. Deleuzian aesthetics, with its ideas of multiplicities, intensities and 'becoming', has had important implications for media, network and cultural theory. It is truly original but can it be applied to art? I experimented with this question in my next body of paintings in which I attempted to convey the aesthetic realization of these ideas.

How complicated and ambiguous it turned out to be, and how many different levels of meaning resulted from this change in my work. It is difficult to stay focused and true to your aesthetic when you are in the milieu of radical intellectuals who are critical of what you are doing. If one is unconsciously motivated, how easy it is to be swayed, impressed and drawn to people and situations which end up having a negative effect on your work, your recognition, the assertion of your identity and the expression of a unique point of view. In 1978, when my work was being recognized in shows at the Whitney and Guggenheim Museums, when I had achieved a more mature style in my painting, the critique of the French radical intellectuals became more intense. Suddenly I turned away from this way of working. To prevent making a centered image I broke the canvas up into a diptych. The earlier application of layers of paint by palette knife now became loosely brushed strokes of paint spread across the canvas. Instead of magical and mysterious shapes, figures, letters, dots and lines were scattered pell-mell. I used dots which formed a loose grid and ruled vertical lines so that they functioned as non-connotative elements. As such, the lines and dots formed abstract images so that no shape should occupy the center of the canvas.

The switch involved a change from a more concentrated focus on archetypal images with their multiple levels of meanings to a more dispersed form of expressiveness. What happened under the influence of *Semiotext(e)* had changed my aesthetic. Nevertheless, as my work took a different turn, and even without the use of an archetypal image, I gradually found a way to convey a great deal of what I had formulated before.

A further change came after revisiting Australia and seeing the Aboriginal art works from Groote Eylandt. Travels to China, Bali, Sri Lanka and South India followed. And there I discovered the Kathakali dance. This dance had an important influence on my work which will be discussed more fully in another chapter. Unknown to me at the time, aesthetic traditions found outside the Western world would resuscitate my own aesthetic and become part of the metonymic process that had earlier stemmed from the influence of Joel Shapiro.

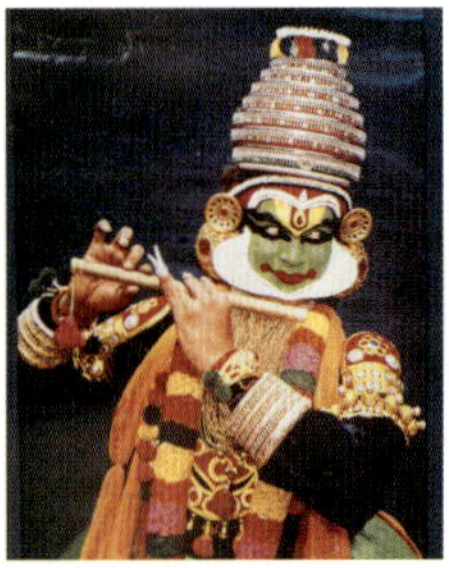

Anonymous Kathakali Dancer, *Lord Krishna Plays His Flute*. Colour photograph, Gurukulam Kathakali, Yogam, Cochin, India.

Notes

1 From the prospectus of a proposed course by Isabelle Mullet and Rachel Wimpee.

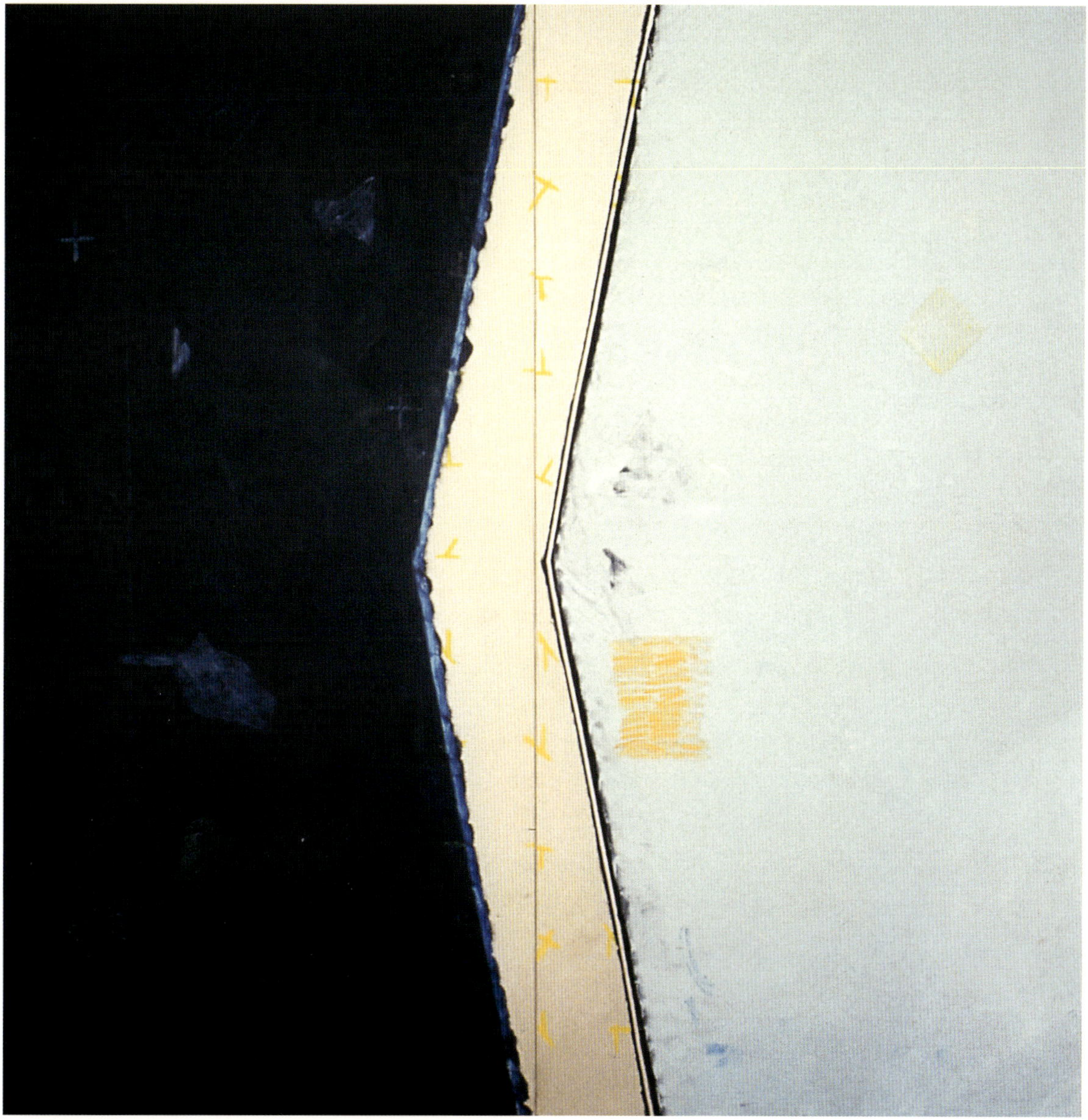

Denise Green, *Nine Degrees*, 1979. Oil and wax stick on canvas, 213 x 213 cm, diptych.

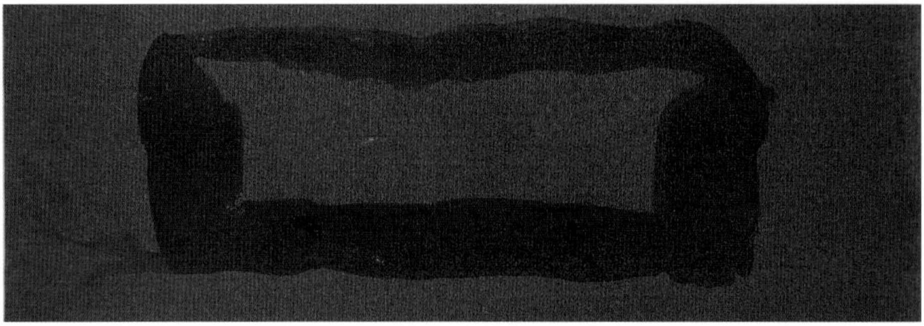

Mark Rothko, *Untitled*, (model for Tate Gallery installation), 1969. Tempera on coloured construction paper, 6.3 x 16.5 cm. © 2005 Kate Rothko Prizel & Christopher Rothko/Artists' Right Society (ARS), New York.

Chapter 5

Robert Motherwell: On Mark Rothko

DG: Was Rothko involved in 'dialogue' with other artists, or did he work in isolation?

RM: On one side he was a very alienated person but then on the other, he saw more artists on a casual basis than any artist I've known. He was always deeply involved with a few intimate friendships. One was with Clyfford Still, which broke up quite early. Another was with Barnett Newman which broke up several years later and one was with me – which lasted with fervor until at least the last two years of his life, when he was half out of his mind with drugs, alcohol and fright.

He had a strongly paranoid streak. It came about partly from being an immigrant and partly from his experiences on the WPA in the 1930s. He regarded the latter with horror for I gather there were strong Marxist pressures exerted on those projects in New York. Abstract artists were not particularly welcomed; they were denied good positions and they felt isolated among their fellow artists. Interestingly, I was the only one in that group who made a political statement in painting and I wasn't on the WPA. But I was never subject to a trauma which made me withdraw totally from a political position. Yet, if you look at the evidence, Rothko signed leftist manifestos throughout his life. I think this was out of fright; or a fear of alienating people within a milieu that he valued.

If he felt at ease with you, he would explode at moments and say what he really thought. But he also tried very consciously to be tactful and to put nothing in writing. His letters are quite impersonal and uninteresting. He didn't want to be nailed; he didn't want to leave any evidence because he had an acute sense of how people can be hanged. So, here was this person behaving with enormous discretion and awareness of a whole world of judges and executioners, but at the same time someone who was very vital, intelligent, emotional, sensitive, volcanic – and sometimes brutal. His daily life might be described as an effort to control, very discreetly, an unbridled rage.

DG: I gather from what you say that he needed to make sense of his personal history and perhaps, therefore, his politics had a private framework.

RM: No, his politics were expedient. But he was like Franz Kafka, to whom the outside world was unreal. Because of its unintelligibility it seemed to Rothko to be devastatingly dangerous. His alienation was total, yet he spent more effort than anybody – except maybe Newman who was equally paranoid – on coming to terms with this strange outside world.

DG: Did his family support him in his effort to make art?

RM: Not at all. In fact, I remember going through months with him, when his mother was dying, deliberating about whether he should or should not go back to Portland to see her. Then, when she died, he wondered whether he should go to the funeral or not. These questions preoccupied, or obsessed, him for months. Sometimes, after we had been talking for a long time, and when he was somewhat drunk, he'd warm up and become revealing – which he always regretted afterwards. He could also get quite repetitious when he became obsessed with some event that had happened to him or about something he had read. One of the memories that frequently recurred in his conversation was about being reared in Czarist Russia. There was anguished contempt, or disdain, but it is difficult to describe exactly what concerned him. He would sometimes become inarticulate and then he would describe what happened when they emigrated to America from a little Russian town. Russian Jews thought American boys must dress in a certain way, so the tailor made him a corduroy suit. After arriving in New York the family travelled across America by train to his relatives in Portland, Oregon. It was there that he realized that the suit was all wrong and he felt humiliated. The anguish and hurt persisted but was often accompanied by roars of laughter.

The closest person to him (they even looked alike) was Groucho Marx – if you can imagine Groucho being highly cultivated and dealing with ultimate concerns. There was a similar mixture of brilliance, quickness and irony. And yet, if Mark were visiting England as a guest and treated with that English grace, tears would come to his eyes when he talked about how civilized and generous the English were.

DG: Perhaps he was not reconciled to his early experience?

RM: That is right. He could be a figure out of Russian or Jewish literature. I know when he was young he wanted to be a cantor. Mozart was his favorite composer and he would sing Mozart sometimes, but it was intoned as if in a Jewish religious service. Certainly, if he had any character resemblance, it would be much more likely to be to Beethoven rather than to Mozart. Mozart was the very opposite – with his Austrian grace, vivacity and spontaneity. Yet Beethoven had the advantage of being a technical genius. What all of us lacked as painters – with the exception of Gorky and de Kooning – was real traditional virtuosity. Consequently, we did not have the confidence that a technical prodigy could have – and at the same time we were trying to work on the level of ultimate concern.

It was obvious that American art of the 1930s was shallow and superficial and that we were now doing more consequential things. What was not so obvious was whether we were succeeding, since there were no standards, except for an idealization of the greatest twentieth century art in Europe. Part of the force of Abstract Expressionism was that at that precise moment we took on the idealism of the first third of the twentieth century in Europe – that same idealism that had already collapsed in Europe. The great art of Europe after the war was made by men who were already masters before the war.

DG: Is it possible for an artist to know who his audience will be? It seems that in the earlier part of Rothko's career, his audience was a small number of fellow artists and then later there was a far wider audience. Did Rothko expect that this would happen?

RM: I think he knew it. But what an artist can't control is the timing. Everybody knew that he was very disappointed at the time of his retrospective in Europe, in 1962,

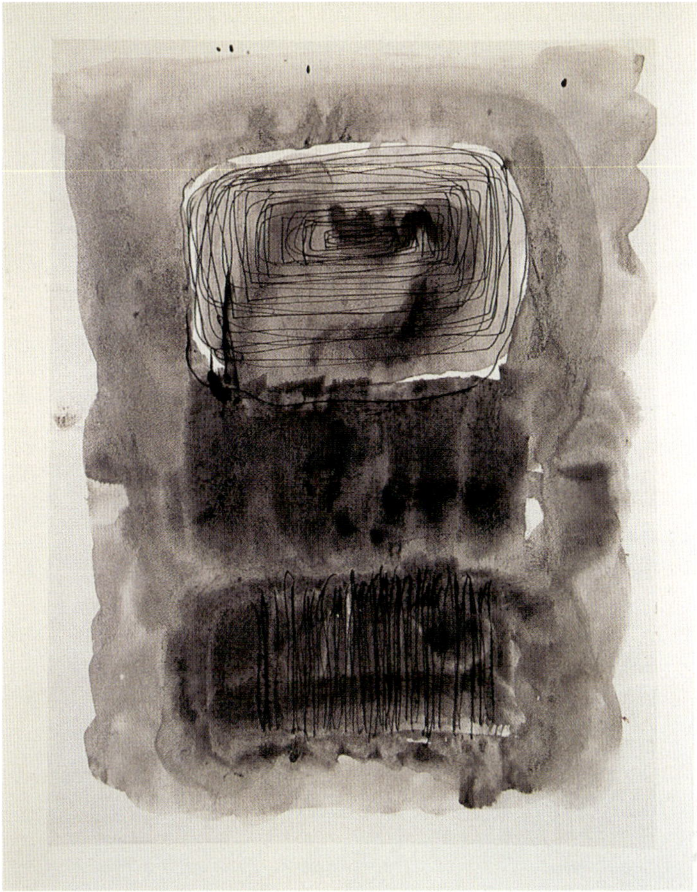

when the French displayed his work in galleries below street level and even closed the show for a while because of heating problems. This was at the height of de Gaullism, and there was French resentment that Paris was not still the queen of the art world. Mark certainly must have known that if the power of the French was behind him he would have been justifiably recognized as one of the greatest world artists to have emerged after World War II.

On the other hand, I think part of his last work, which is markedly different from his main mature style, was influenced by the possibility of a commission from UNESCO. It was to do a room in Paris, along with Giacometti sculptures.

Mark Rothko, *Untitled*, 1961. Pen and ink on paper, 28 x 21.5 cm. © 2005 Kate Rothko Prizel & Christopher Rothko/Artists' Rights Society (ARS), New York.

He began with small paintings on paper which ultimately became black and grey and more geometric. I think he was conscious that these paintings would be shown with Giacometti sculptures and he wanted to make Abstract Expressionist equivalents of the same tone.

He would go to many shows, perhaps twelve in a week, and he would listen to everything everyone was saying – drawing his own conclusions. What is wrong with the Romantic myth is the idea that art is made by individuals, whereas I think it is a collective thing. The supremely great artists – such as Homer, Shakespeare, Mozart or Johann Sebastian Bach – were all performers and in direct contact with their audience. I don't think it's possible to reach that level of greatness without being immediately in contact with one's audience. Mark used to go to openings, look at the pictures, and listen to what people were saying. He combined what he learned with his own intelligence and a sense of profound integrity. He used to sum it up in one sentence, 'A picture is good if you can endure it'.

He used to say no-one understood how aggressive his works were. Rothko not only learned a lot from all those openings, but he was defending himself against the envy of the art scene by being the only major artist to appear at previews. He was shrewd perhaps – full of cunning.

DG: Did Rothko and say, Jackson Pollock, have a friendly relationship with Peggy Guggenheim?

RM: I'm sure not. They didn't fit that milieu at all, which was very French, Parisian, international, sophisticated. The Surrealists, Chagall and George Grosz were more sophisticated than Mark, and less profound. Mark had no social graces. He didn't make small conversation. He didn't dress well. In fact, for years I used to give him my suits, without embarrassment, because he accepted them without embarrassment. They were probably better suits, both in quality and taste, than anything he'd find for himself. I've heard that during the depression days he used to buy his suits from funeral parlors for $2.00 or $3.00. Although young artists now have their own struggles, they have no conception of the world we faced.

DG: A young artist today has to move in and out of different social contexts, which doesn't encourage risk-taking.

RM: We could take tremendous risks because in those days nobody gave a damn what we did. So, in a sense we weren't part of the scene at all. We were our own scene, like retarded children in a separate room and the rest of the school didn't care at all what we did.

DG: Was Rothko analysed?

RM: No, I used to implore him to do so, but he had an absolute hostility towards the idea. While he read very few things, when he did so it was very carefully and he never forgot what he read. At my suggestion, he read Freud's *Totem and Taboo* and it made an indelible impression on him. Another book that impressed him was *The Golden Bough* by Sir James Frazer. It begins by introducing the old priest guarding the golden bough and describing how any young priest who could assassinate the old priest would become the new guardian. Then he, in turn, would have to guard against all the younger ones who were hiding and waiting for their moment of opportunity. Mark used to regard teaching like that. He would say, why do you teach all these potential rivals who are going to kill you. He used to say the same things about the club, on the Friday evenings.

DG: Why did Rothko feel such hostility against the idea of being analysed when so many members of your generation were analysed?

RM: I don't think he could have been analysed. He was too old, and in a funny kind of way, too intelligent. He would have regarded the analyst as an opponent, as everybody does in the beginning. But he never would have relented on that. Which is to say that a person can't be analysed unless they are brought to their knees. Mark had to control, I think, even his own death. He would have chosen to kill himself rather than waiting around for God to decide the moment and the circumstances. With that kind of attitude, a person can't be analysed. Mark was incapable of dialogue. He was capable of listening, and the more anguished your story, the more moved and sympathetic he was. But our relationship was always best when I was brought to my knees. Always worst when I was riding high. He could speak of his own feelings very articulately, but there was no dialectical development in our conversation.

DG: You said in an article once that it is important to discover or establish one's identity – that this was the American's experience. It seems that for an American, establishing an identity means engaging in some kind of dialogue, and frequently participating in group or community situations.

RM: Then I should qualify what I said by saying that Mark did engage in a dialogue on a 'family' basis. This means that he and I, and Barnett Newman, Bradley Tomlin, Herbert Ferber and Nikos Stamos were sort of Mark's adopted family. We had a very intimate dialogue about ordinary daily life. We celebrated each other's birthdays, lent each other money, talked about where to live and what to do when we weren't working. But the dialogue was never about the world of the spirit. Basically, we were a clan, or a family that happened to be made up of painters.

DG: There are a number of different ways to engage in dialogue. Usually the artist has a dialogue with his self and his fictive self. And then there's the possibility of another dialogue which is critical, or self-conscious – a reflection back on the artist's activity – which can take place with another person or outsiders. Did this take place within the family situation which you describe?

RM: I don't know how many times I was in Rothko's studio and never once saw a brush or a can of paint. Very often the pictures would be faced to the wall. There would be no evidence of how they were made. He was very reluctant to talk about what medium he used, what colours, or what kind of brushes. I finally figured it out by encountering it in my own experiments with this and that. I discovered that a stiff house-painter's brush, if you hold it in a certain way, automatically makes that feathery edge. He made his own stretchers because of poverty, and by turning the wood sideways he could use quite thin, inexpensive wood, like lathe, and make a stretcher that was strong enough. I personally believe that the paintings from his mature phase – what we call the Rothko image – were originally in egg tempera. They have a surface quality that one doesn't do easily in oil. Toward the end he experimented with acrylics.

DG: The literature that surrounds Rothko's retrospective in 1961 frequently tended to see him as a mystic. It seems quite clear that this wasn't his situation, yet the paintings do function as some kind of revelation.

RM: Penguin has published a book called *Ecstatic Religion* and there is a chapter on shamans and a lot of discussion about the person who becomes the witchdoctor or magician in the tribe. What interests me very much is that the shaman very often doesn't want to be the shaman, but it's the collective

Mark Rothko, *Untitled*, 1967. Acrylic on paper mounted on Masonite, 60.5 x 48 x 3.9 cm.

judgement of the tribe that that's the person who is most in touch with the spirits. That happened to Mark. In many ways he didn't want to be the shaman, yet he could act like one. I've seen him with important collectors and dealers and his capacity to fill another with awe and a sense of privilege at seeing his work was incredible.

DG: It sounds as if he had a sense of the theatricality of the situation, although I don't mean to demean it.

RM: Ritual is the word he would have used. This was something that was very deep in him and caused a bond between him and Newman. He was always hurt by the break between them. I've turned more and more to what I call atavistic art. Stonehenge interests me, or Altamira or the Vikings and I think, from another angle, Mark was more interested in Tartar tents or the flow of the green and red lantern in a chemist shop at night in a dark street. Also something very atavistic.

DG: There's a show of drawings at the Guggenheim Museum now which included two watercolours and several panels by Rothko. How did drawing function in Rothko's work?

RM: He used to claim, and I think it might have been true in the beginning, but I don't think it was in the end, that all his mature work began with doodling.The biomorphic period, or surrealist period of the early 1940s is concerned with drawing and I can imagine the later paintings coming about by cancelling out certain areas. I've never seen a drawing by him. One of his trustees saw one and said it was very much after Picasso in its influence. Mark used to say he hated Cubism. Like many Americans of that generation, he was very concerned to cover his tracks, and to have American art seem to be a virgin birth. That shocked the scholar in me.

The one thing we did talk about was 'edge'. Some corny artist said somewhere that all the technical problems in painting are basically how the edges meet. I enforced that conversation and Mark was very interested. We used to talk a lot about it – it's the only technical thing I can remember talking about. But I think he had a very poor sense of scale in the sense that he could not use just any scale. He worked to a scale in which he functioned perfectly, but if he worked larger or smaller than that, it ceased to function.

DG: Rothko planned a series of paintings for the Seagram Building, but this didn't work out.

RM: Philip Johnson commissioned Mark to make the painting for the Four Seasons Restaurant, which Mark did. But the idea of businessmen discussing business in front of them sickened him and he refused to deliver them. So, he gave them to Harvard, where they hang in the Faculty Dining Room. There, the professors talk in front of them, equally ignoring them. You can imagine how excited he was at the idea of a chapel, which was a situation where they would be objects of meditation.

I will say point blank that he was a real hero, but you have to remember also that he was paranoid and by definition very sensitive to other people's opinions and he never had that machine going for him that, say, de Kooning or Pollock did.

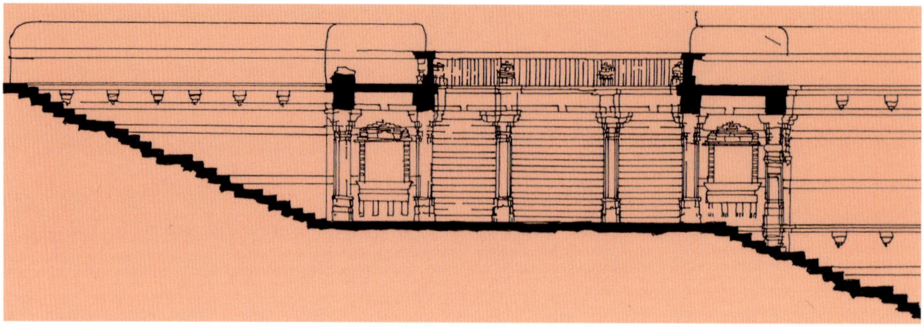

Elevation of section of a Stepwell at Adalaj, India. Re-drawn by Carolina Rosensztroch.

Chapter 6

The 1980s: Asia and its Influence. The Indian Experience

My experience in India proved to be a counterweight to many of the artistic and intellectual trends dominant in the New York art world at the end of the 1970s. Unlike the art world in the West, which is concerned with the avant-garde and ultimately values the new, what I found in India was an honouring of ancient traditions. There are three important experiences through which I realised my encounter with India differed from my immersion in American and European culture. The Kathakali dance, the social spectacle of colour and the geometry of the stepwells in the state of Gujarat were constant sources of stimulation that opened new imaginary domains for me.

Kathakali is a performance of dance and pantomime drama that originated in the temples of Kerala in South India over 2000 years ago. Drawn from the Hindu epics of the Ramayana and the Mahabharata, the philosophy behind the dance is a form of yoga. It takes place out of doors and lasts a whole night. What impressed me was how ancient it was and how this could be sensed through the vivid and elaborate costumes, the green faces, the language of gesticulation and the crowns and head-dresses. How startled I was to see the facial painting and the whites of the eyes turned to deep red. The make-up was so elaborate it appeared almost as if the characters were wearing masks. But the skin is painted so that the spectator is captivated by the grimaces and facial expressions. The eyes were the focus of attention for the mouth stayed closed throughout the whole performance and seemed to be stretched into a grin.

All the dancers were male, though they often portrayed female characters. I remember the spectacular physical presence of the character known as The Evil (Red Beard). He had a black face and an extraordinarily exaggerated red beard. Two large fangs descended below a white moustache that extended out past his ears. He wore a crown of stacked domes. I was close enough to observe his gestures in

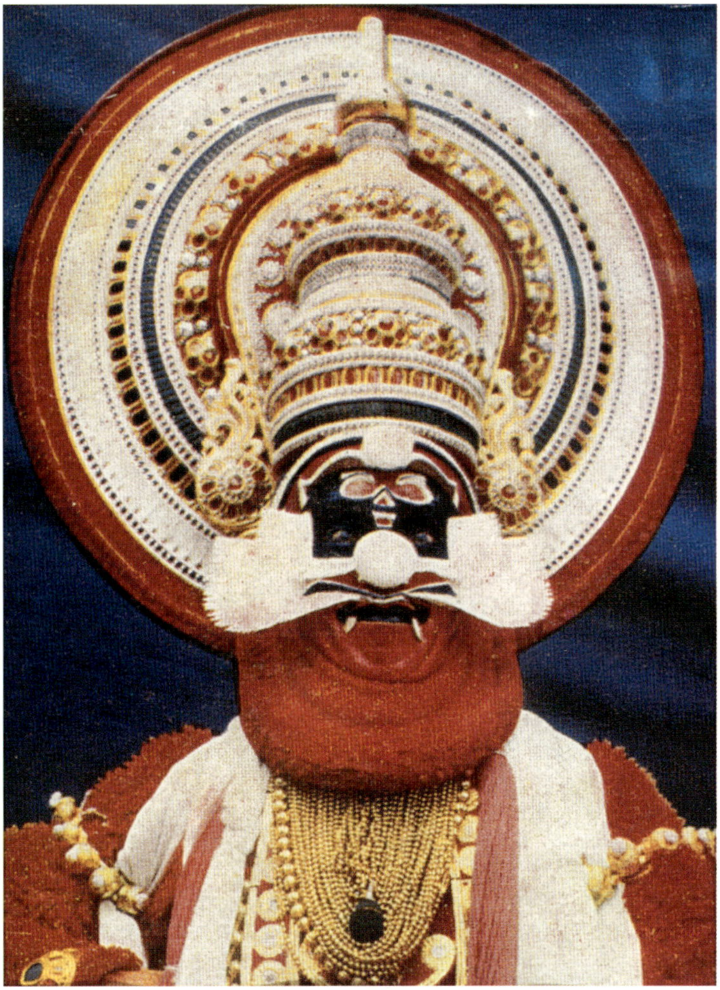

Anonymous, Kathakali Dancer, *The Evil (Red Beard).* Colour photograph, Gurukulam Kathakali, Yogam, Cochin, India.

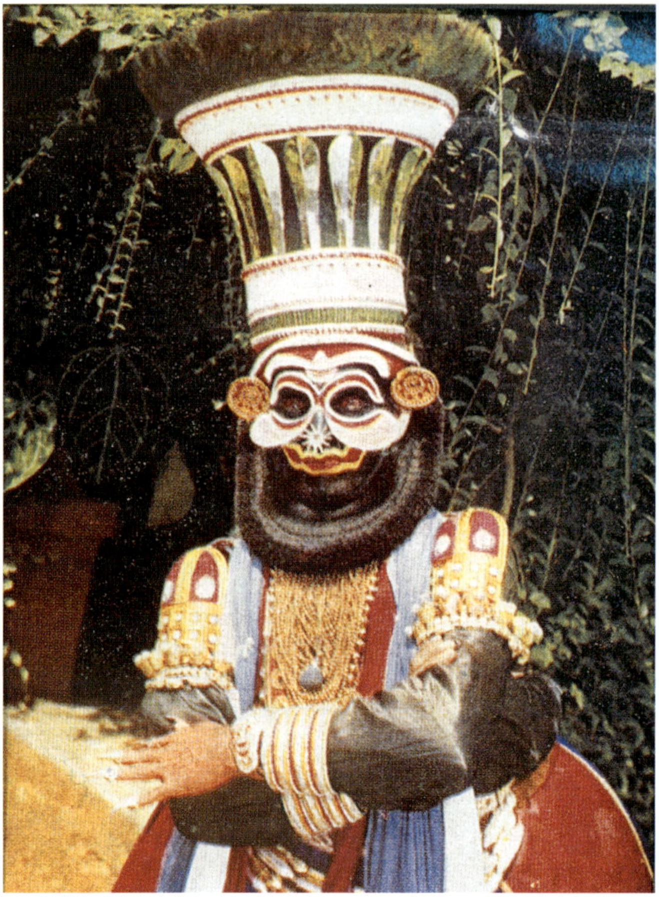

Anonymous, Kathakali Dancer, ***Black Beard.*** **Colour photograph, Gurukulam Kathakali, Yogam, Cochin, India.**

detail, the rolling eyes and facial movements and his pounding and stomping feet. The Evil (Red Beard) was a fearful being. He twirled and made a racket with the bells on his upper arms. Most curious of all was the imposing girth of the character. All the costumes were voluminous and doubled the size of the dancers.

The experience of the dance made me feel that instead of witnessing everyday figures, as on the Western stage, these were larger than life, mythic figures. It was as if I were in the presence of demonic and divine beings. Although the Kathakali tradition functions as a form of religious theatre, I related to it as art and the kind of aesthetic that attracted me. It stirred me to want to paint and inspired my return to Kerala the following year to spend more time in the presence of this art form.

The second source of stimulation came from the social spectacle of colour. The light I remember was a humid summer whiteness. The men, too, were all in white. They wore soft robes of light-weight, paper-thin fabric, which gave a sense of a veiled body. The weight of the fabric added to one's awareness of the body, its warmth and solidity. It contributed to the beauty and sensuousness of the men, and emphasised the elegance and purity of their dress.

My eye was hypnotized by the women moving slowly through the streets; to Western eyes, a spectacle of goddesses. I loved the full-length saris and imagined that only the lower caste women wore the brightest and most spectacular colours – perhaps a blouse with a combination of bold yellow orange and fuchsia pink and a dark green skirt with an orange band around the hem. Their arms were heavy with bracelets, from the wrist to the elbow and then all the way up the upper arm. I was seeing a different sensibility. Here were sumptuous and breathtaking images, differentiated by the use of pure colour, and I found them fascinating. They were something beautiful, different and to be respected. In the dress I saw a new aesthetic with a cultural dimension that expressed a notion of inner self unlike that of people in the West where women dressed stylishly to convey privilege and self esteem.

The mere fact of seeing women carrying stacked copper vessels on their heads was astounding and spectacular. Other women carried large flat platters. They walked with a slow gait. In the cities enormous crowds walked in the streets, along with bicycles, motorized rickshaws, occasional cars, cows and sometimes camels and motorcycles. But all wove their way forward, without colliding.

What struck me most were the images of women wearing saris of one colour. A woman might wear pure green, with the fabric softly draped over her head and down to the feet. As she sat or walked she would become a simple shape presented in a pure, saturated hue. There in the street, or at a railway station, I would see women grouped together, each wearing a jewel-coloured sari and ornaments in her hair. Each sari was rich and varied. I enjoyed the different traditions of dress and found the colours a source of visual pleasure. Indeed it was not unlike the experience of moving through a museum and enjoying the gems of an artistic tradition. The sight of the women and their saris was equivalent to savoring the unique world view or sensibility of artists like Bonnard, Rothko or Noland.

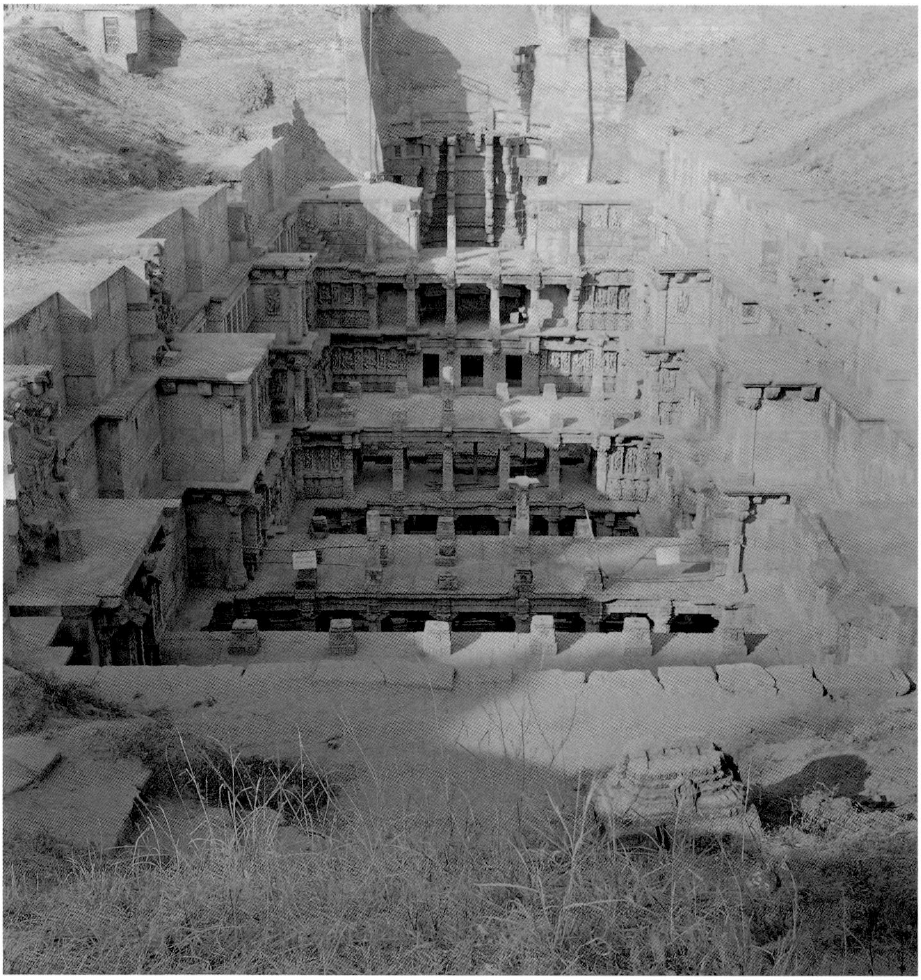

Morna Livingstone,
***Patan, Gujarat*, 1986.**
Stepwell photographs.

first published in *Steps to Water: The Ancient Stepwells of India*,
Princeton Architectural Press, 2003.

The third way in which India influenced me was through the ornate and elaborate architecture of the stepwells and stepped ponds in the state of Gujarat. The geometry in these staired structures was complex and striking and, like everything else in India, related to religion. The Gujarati builders employed an ancient design concept, called *vedha*, which called for a high degree of bilateral symmetry to make a building auspicious.[1]

The first site I visited was a stepped pond located in the open air, adjacent to the Hindu Sun Temple at Modhera. The well is configured as a huge rectangle that is at least 150 feet on its longer side. It is like an inverted pyramid that penetrates deep into the ground down to the water level. Lateral steps on all four sides form endless pathways to the water, with another smaller set of steps set at a diagonal perpendicular to the lateral steps. The steps and their landings establish sacred positions for the devotees and are derived from the cosmic importance of numbers. Interspersed among the stairs are shrines and niches with carvings of deities.

But for me the most impressive site was the 15th century stepwell Adalaj Vava, at the town also called Adalaj. I was told to go there by Anand Sarabhai. He knew I would see something that was ancient and yet had a modernist sensibility. After seeing it I felt that I needed to read more about it, just to know what I had seen. It was like a mirage. There you are in the desert which is hot and dry – not totally arid, but not far from it. Then suddenly, without confronting an imposing monument or large edifice, you find yourself visiting a major architectural site – and it is all below ground level. The three entrances are flanked by pairs of miniature buildings (*todas*), no taller than a person. By descending the stairs the visitor is led through a structure nine stories deep, which shifts from an open octagon at the top to a square at its base.[2] Each level has open rooms, often supported by ornate columns. While descending level by level, a sequence of these chambers is observed.

The open well-shaft is the central area of the structure and at the bottom there is water which people can drink. Visitors find themselves in a space composed of repeating room-like pavilions. They are cave-like spaces with ledges, balcony railings and columns. The carved and ornate columns give the spaces an openness and lightness, and the experience is quite unlike being in an enclosed and locked-in space. I experienced the aesthetic dimension of these spaces. In New York I had been aware of the minimal structures of Sol LeWitt and Don Judd, with their geometric permutations. I could relate the experience of Adalaj Vava to their aesthetic, but even more so to the music of Phil Glass with its slow transformations and repeating arpeggiated chordal figures.

Apart from serving important ritual purposes,[3] the stepwells also combine an aesthetic experience of complex and striking geometry with the social function of providing people with a protected, cool space in which to mingle. The tremendous beauty of this abstract structure belies the fact that it serves a practical purpose – to

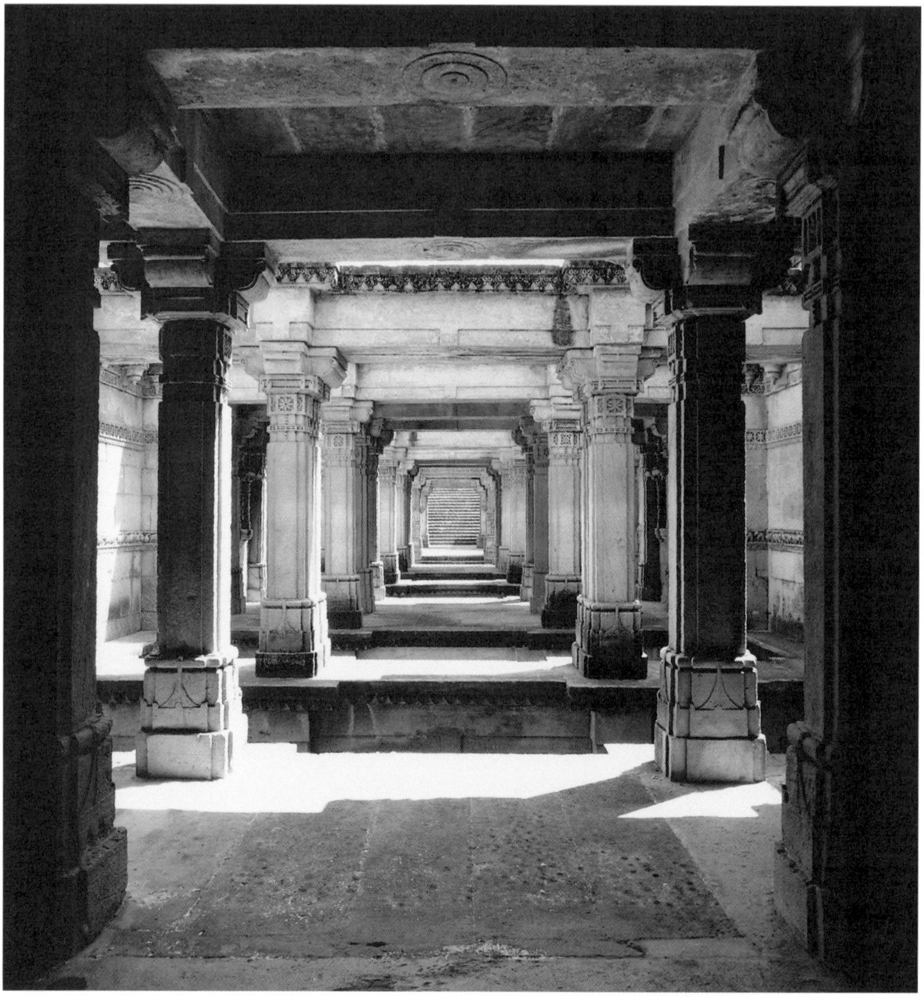

Morna Livingstone, *Adalaj, View Through Pavilion*, 1986. Black and white photograph. © 2005 Morna Livingstone.

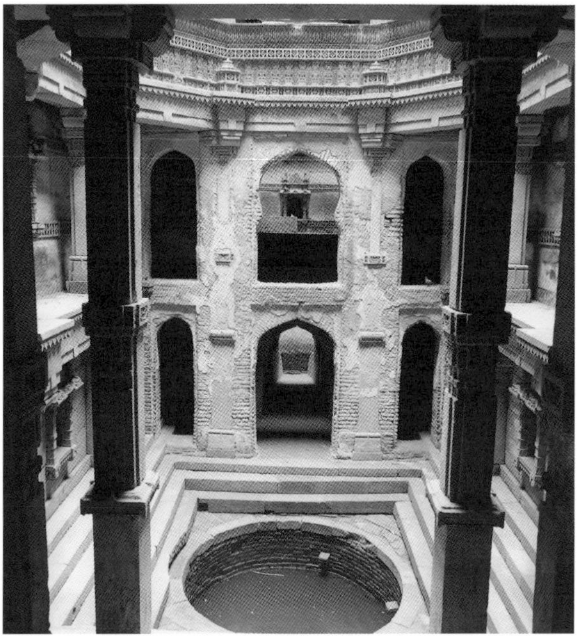

give people access to water and shelter from the sun and heat.

How did the encounter with India impact on my work? In retrospect, I can see how my paintings opened themselves up to rich colour, markings and an exploration of abstract line and touch. Although not interested in making a figurative representation of the architecture or the dance, several paintings from that year refer directly to the colour of the faces of the dancers. I had broken the painting into a diptych, separating the two panels with a curved line. In my painting *Moreover*, the left half of the painting is red and the right half black. This element was borrowed from the face of one of the dance characters who had a line going from the bridge of his nose to the lobe of his ear. The upper part of the face was black and the lower red. The green face of the character Lord Krishna is referenced in another painting entitled *Scans*.

Because I had been deeply impressed by the mythic dimension of the figures, I attempted to translate this feeling into my paintings. It became distilled through abstract elements, including the size of the paintings, which jumped from a five to a seven foot square format. While the epic narrative of the dance was dramatized

Morna Livingstone, *Approaching the Pool, Adalaj*, 1986. Black and white photograph. © 2005 Morna Livingstone.

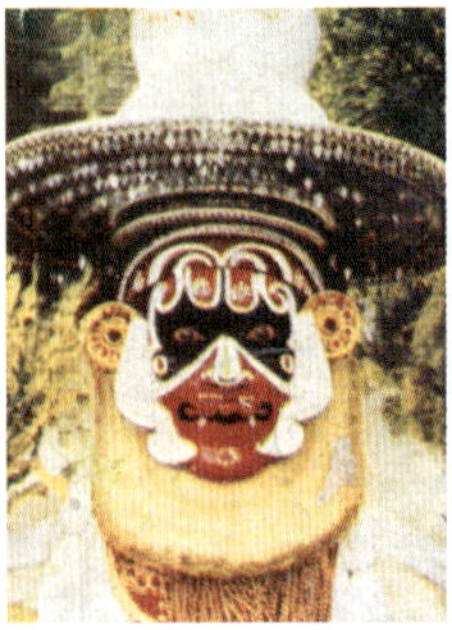

through facial expressions and gestures of the hands (*mudras*), embedded in the paintings were symbols such as small fan shapes, pointing fingers, and an eye-ball or lips. Although it was not my intent at the time, I realized much later that there was a metonymic process at work here. The larger size of the canvas and the geometric image of the curved line at its center were intuitive ways of manifesting the mythic presence of the figures and its impact on me.

My affinity with this ancient art form differed from the way artists in the early part of the last century were influenced by tribal art. Inspired by African masks and sculptures, Picasso and Braque incorporated the outer and formal aspects into their work. But these objects were also empowered by magical properties. They shared a spiritual dimension not unlike that of the Kathakali dance, which was manifested through the artist's inner state of consciousness. It was this spiritual aspect that attracted me and became a powerful influence on my later work.

In 1984 I began scattering lines over the surfaces of the paintings and introduced squares, circles and quadrants. The stepwells and their complex spatial ambiguities reinforced the presence of an underlying geometric structure in my work so that I could then freely play with colour. The painting, *Intimacy*, has a square at the center

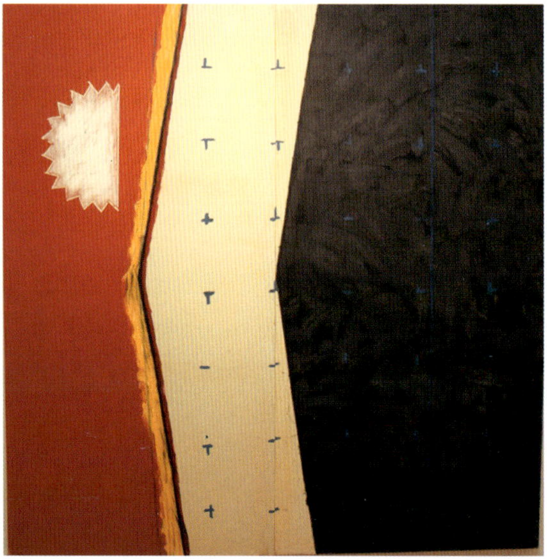

Above:
Anonymous, Kathakali Dancer. Colour photograph. Gurukulam Kathakali, Yogam, Cochin, India.

Right:
Denise Green, *More Over*, 1979. Oil on canvas, 213 x 213 cm, diptych. Photograph: Nicholas Walster.

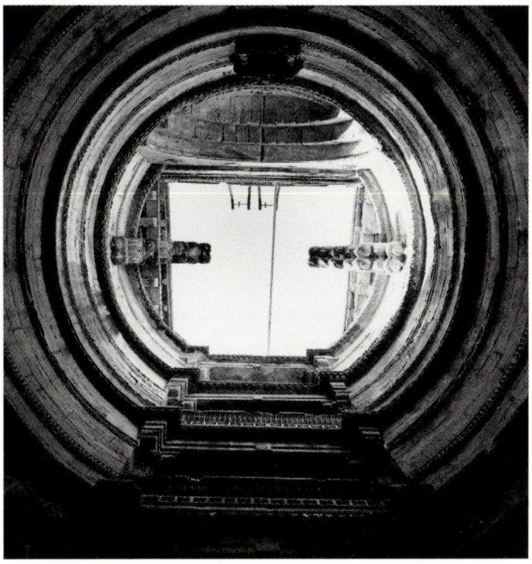

and larger concentric circles surrounding it, reminiscent of looking up at the sky from the cylinder of the well. It is painted in a deep indigo blue with white lines for the circles.

Early in 1986 a whole other facet of my work evolved. I had the opportunity of creating work in Ahmedabad, having been invited by the Sarabhais, a distinguished family and patrons of the arts, to stay with them and work on a paper-making project at the Gandhi Ashram. I responded to the stimulus of working on site and a profusion of colours entered the work. Arriving at the gates of the Sarabhai compound, one follows a red sienna dirt road shaded and protected by large trees. At the front of Manibhai Sarabhai's home stands the elephant statue of Ganesh, the god who paves the way for all endeavours. Ahmedabad was a center of textile mills and the Ashram had been Gandhi's residence for 20 years. Following his basic principle of recycling, the scraps from the mills were brought to the Ashram where they were converted into pulp and then into superior quality rag paper. The paper-making process was a new technique for me and it was a challenging project. But I had the help of master paperworkers and produced a suite of 126 works in just three weeks. Due to the nature of the technique, I was involved with an improvisation under water.

The pulp would be poured into large vats of water and spread evenly within a wood frame with a mesh screen underneath. The screen was then lifted out of the

Left:
Denise Green, *Intimacy*, 1986. Oil, wax, paint stick on canvas, 169 x 169 cm. Photograph: Nicholas Walster.

Right:
Morna Livingstone, *View up into the Adalaj Cylinder*, 1965. Black and white photograph. © 2005 Morna Livingstone.

water and the colour, shapes and markings would be freely added to the surface. Since there were no chemicals available to fix the colours, I had to come up with various ways to try to control their spread. The challenge of this technical problem led to a new freedom and openness to chance. Sometimes I placed a large, metal geometric mould on the surface and filled it with coloured pulp. At other times I drew freely with coloured pulp directly onto the screen. When the improvisations were completed, the screen would be wrapped in burlap and passed through a pressing machine to consolidate the paper and eliminate the water. This final pressing would cause dramatic and unexpected shifts of colour and design.

In contrast to my paintings, the paper works made at the Gandhi Ashram had to be more spontaneous. I was working in a different medium which involved the breaking of habits of thinking in the creative process. I was also responding to the visual stimuli of the place and releasing it into the paper. In many works the black seeped out of its borders diffusing itself into a soft gray that expanded to the edges of the paper. By letting go of my usual habits and connections I was able to be more open to the uncontrollable spread of colour which was India itself.

Understanding India

While in India I recognized that many things in the culture were radically different from their counterparts in the West. But I had to return to New York to understand my experience. I became familiar with the writings of the linguist and folklorist A.K. Ramanujan, especially his essay 'Is there an Indian Way of Thinking? An Informal Essay'. Another discovery was the work of the psychoanalyst Alan Roland and his book *In Search of Self in India and Japan: Toward a Cross Cultural Psychology*. Through these writings I was introduced to the Hindu philosophy of monism which emphasizes the continuum between self and other and mind and body – in strong contrast to the Cartesian dualisms of Western thought. My understanding of the idea of metonymic thinking followed. It tied into my own experience in India.

While reading Roland and Ramanujan in New York, I had the opportunity to see the statue of Uma, the goddess of creative power and energy, which is described in my chapter on Benjamin. Now I could see it not only in a Western symbolic way but in an Eastern way too. If you apply an Indian or metonymic way of thinking about it, then this carving is not so much a symbol of the deity, rather it is a partial embodiment of the

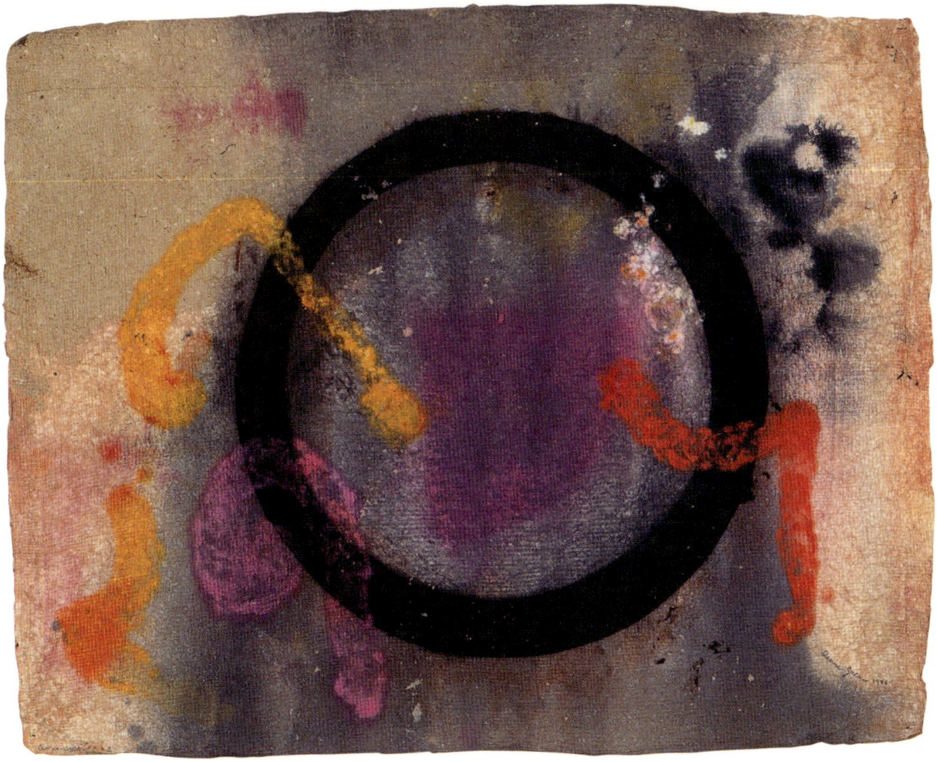

creative forces of power and energy.

But the writings of Roland and Ramanujan made me aware that when the emphasis is on the metonymic, it is not only the mode of appreciation that is different, but the process of creation as well. When Indian artists carve these sacred figures, they proceed by accessing spiritual states of mind in which there is no separation between the creator and the created object. Western artists use symbolic thinking and maintain the separation between self and object. For Pygmalion it took a divine intervention to make the statue come alive, but for Indian artists art works are actual embodiments of the forces associated with a deity. In 1986 I had visited the Dalwara Temple in Mount Abu, a Jain temple which contained white marble figures of deities called Jinas. Each morning the Jinas were bathed in milk and honey and now I understood why the monks performed this ceremony.

Denise Green, *Surya Chandra 1*, 1986. Indian hand-made paper, dyed, 66 x 84 cm. Collection: Museum of Contemporary Art, Sydney.

The Kathakali dancers also use a metonymic process to create the main mythic characters, both divine and demonic, from the Ramayana and Mahabharata. This entails preparing for the dance by practising spiritual disciplines (*sadhana*), including a long ritual of painting the face and putting on elaborate costumes. For an Indian spectator, using a metonymic way of looking at the drama, the dancers do not portray the characters instead they *become* the characters. For the performers, the dance drama expresses a continuum between their own spiritual state and the spiritual being of the characters.

As I came to understand metonymic thinking in the Indian aesthetic and way of creating I began reflecting on how it occurred in the work of contemporary Western artists. I spoke with Brice Marden in November 1992. This important painter has been influenced by Asia and our conversation reveals how he had independently come up with an idea that is related to the metonymic process.

BM: I made drastic changes a few years ago. Now that I've been working on the changes I understand them more. First you study Western art, then you start studying Eastern art, and then all of that reinforces what you know. But you come out of the study with a whole series of fresh ideas.

DG: What drew you to the new ideas or imagery in your work?

BM: I was drawing from nature, but the drawings were looser than the paintings. I assumed the drawings and the paintings were going to come together. When they didn't, I figured I had to push the process further.

DG: Did you respond to one kind of landscape more than another? Were you drawn more to one kind of natural phenomenon, like trees?

BM: I've been more drawn toward the trees than the landscape space. I'm more interested in picking up the energy, rather than the details of a landscape. I want to transmit that kind of energy that occurs in nature – or rather, my feelings about it. I want to transfer that energy into the paintings.

DG: How do the intuitive changes occur in your work? When they happen do you find it essential to persevere, to see if they are leading somewhere?

BM: Changes in my work are forced, and keep changing as I go along. The forms are now becoming rounder and involved in a different kind of space than originally. This has to do with becoming more acquainted with the material.

DG: After seeing slides of the recent work and the paintings connected to *The Three Graces*, it seemed to me that something more intuitive was emerging.

BM: I've been trying to retain primal subject matter, that is, not to become depictive but to keep certain energies alive. I remember when I was a student, Alex Katz talked about painting the landscape and how trees could be painted as though they were a thousand dancing people. There is a constant shift and flickering. You look at the sea and try to draw the way the water moves; what's happening on the surface reflects what's happening underneath. While more formal work is done in the studio, out in the field you're drawing and observing – just trying to get that movement. One is more formal and the other is more immediate and the two must be pulled together. By working in the area in between you get something going. Then you allow it, or you follow it, or it follows you. It must be natural.

DG: This process is non-verbal and it is hard to put it into words.

BM: Yes. You approach the work very formally, but then it becomes intuitive and ends up being something you didn't expect. I'm always looking to get to that point where I'm losing the formality. I find it difficult to get to that place. The painting part is slower and more deliberate and it takes more time to get to that moment of liberation. When I sit down and start drawing, it's much easier. It's one thing to have your hand moving around, but it's another to be painting on a human scale and achieving that kind of movement or kinaesthesia that I want. It's a matter of kinaesthetic transferral from what's inside the artist onto the paper – as in calligraphy. It is the transferral of energies which I find intriguing. But I find it difficult to have it happen on a human scale. I tend to work more on the scale of de Kooning. I mean, in the de Kooning's you are always aware that you can reach so high and you can reach so wide. You have a real feeling of the artist being in front of the work and making it, whereas with Pollock the artist becomes lost in it.

DG: What attracted you to calligraphy and its energy?

BM: I always felt there was an energy in the colour and forms in the earlier panel paintings. As they became more complex, I tried to get more movement into them and I found I had to explore the monochromatic approach.

DG: When you speak of the energy within the colour of your earlier paintings, are

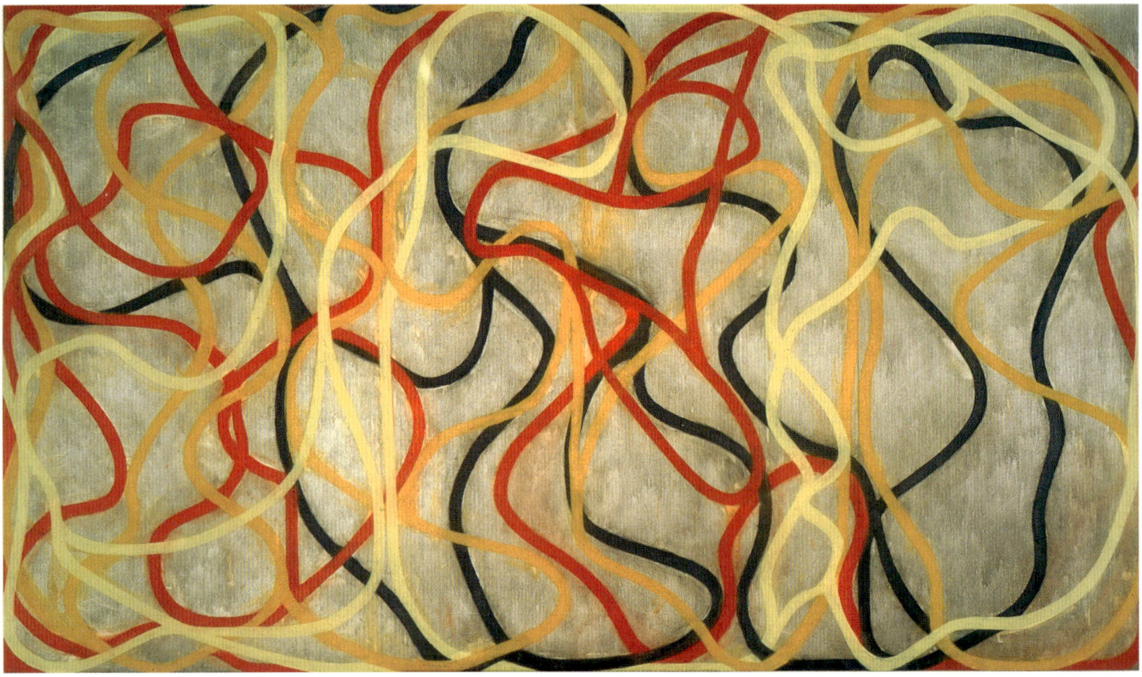

Brice Marden, *Chinese Dancing*, 1994-96. Oil on canvas, 152 x 274 cm. Courtesy of the UBS Collection.

you referring to any particular series of works?

BM: No, although some specific pieces seemed to have a certain presence. It might be enigmatic, but I would always see a shimmering behind them, or somewhere within them. The way the colour holds the plane creates a kind of tension and energy. In the new paintings I want to be able to do this more, so the work has gotten more linear. There hasn't been the same emphasis on colour.

DG: Do the recent paintings relate to yourself in any way? Or were you inspired by your interaction with other artists and other traditions? Does this body of work create a dialogue with Pollock, or with Chinese calligraphy?

BM: I keep thinking I have a real historical orientation in terms of what seems important and enduring. Then, as I continue working, whole chunks of tradition disappear. Ingres just falls out of the picture for me. Right now I am having a difficult time with the idea of any kind of rectangle seen as a window. That perspectival way of approaching space was a limitation that worked on painting for 500 years. Modernist painting is getting away from that tradition, and Asian painting never really cared about it. It is very exciting to see this affirmation of something you always suspected. I see myself as a modernist painter who is involved with ideas about illusion, vision, expression and energy. But I keep thinking that what the painting is, ultimately, is energy. It isn't necessarily mine. It is just energy. You have put it there, but it doesn't exist without somebody else putting their own energy into it. Pollock was the one who had the most energy.

The aspect of Chinese calligraphy that Marden is drawn to is the internal energy (*ch'i*). He refers to this as the 'kinesthetic transferral from what's inside the artist onto the paper'. For the Chinese, creativity is the result of a mobilization of energies in the body itself. *Ch'i* is internal energy and to practise calligraphy is to externalize the energies within oneself. Like the Kathakali dancers who practise their dance as a 'sadhana', Chinese calligraphers trace a dozen calligraphic characters as their spiritual discipline. By practising calligraphic writing they gain a peaceful state of mind and possession of themselves. Marden's process is analogous. The shift in his work was partly driven by his interest in getting more movement into his painting. Marden was inspired by the energy in trees and nature, which he tried to express in his painting by drawing on his own internal energy. There is a metonymic continuity between the energy in nature, the energy within Marden and in the paintings.

In summary, different artists use the metonymic process in somewhat different ways. I use it to externalize internal states; Agnes Martin uses the process in her work to externalize feelings about nature; Ross Bleckner conveys images of light to externalize internal experiences and Brice Marden uses the metonymic process to relate internal energies to those he finds in nature.

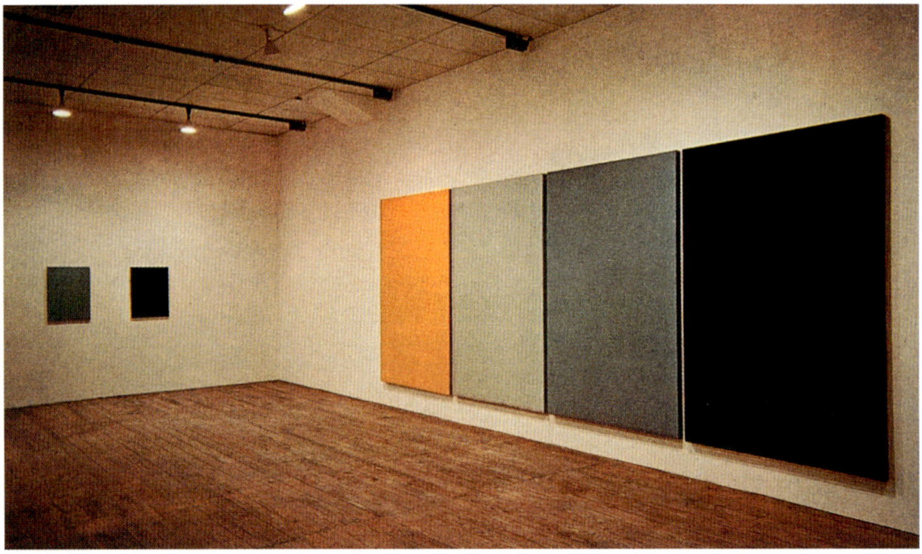

Brice Marden, *Seasons* (right) and two of the four panels of *Seasons – Small Version* (left), installed in the Rice Museum exhibition, April-May 1976.

Notes

1 V.S. Pramar, 1989 *Haveli: Wooden Houses and Mansions of Gujarat,* Ahmedabad: Grantha in association with Mapin, p. 105.

2 Morna Livingston, *Steps to Water. The Ancient Stepwells of India*, Princeton Architectural Press, New York, 2002.

3 Ibid., xi and 31. Stepped ponds are used for ritual bathing related to temple worship and mosque ceremonies. In the stepwells, shrines are made exclusively for ritual, and stairs, landings, pavilions, parapets and the pool all offer surfaces for the improvisation of extra ritual. Marks of pure pigment are made and shiny foil is cut into patterns and pasted on the surface of a rock, a stone, a wall, or a tree. Ritual in the stepwells involves ceremonies called *pujas*, which men and women perform after bathing to honour the deities.

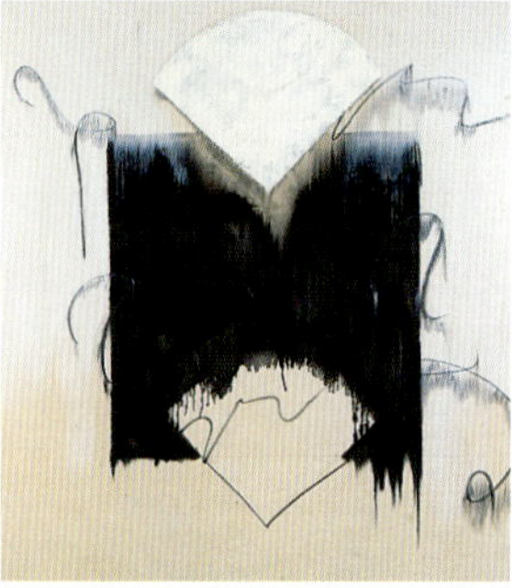 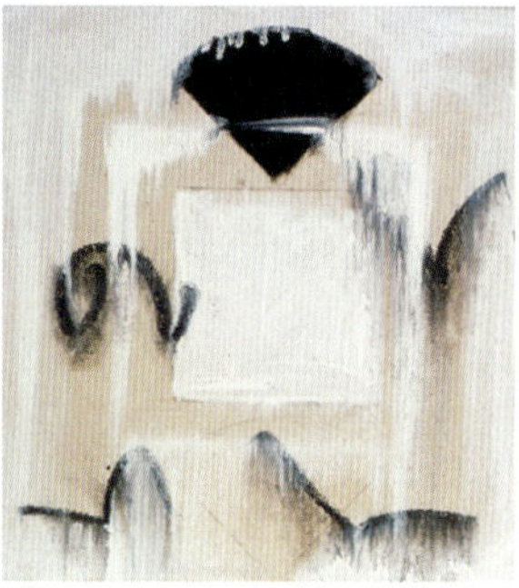 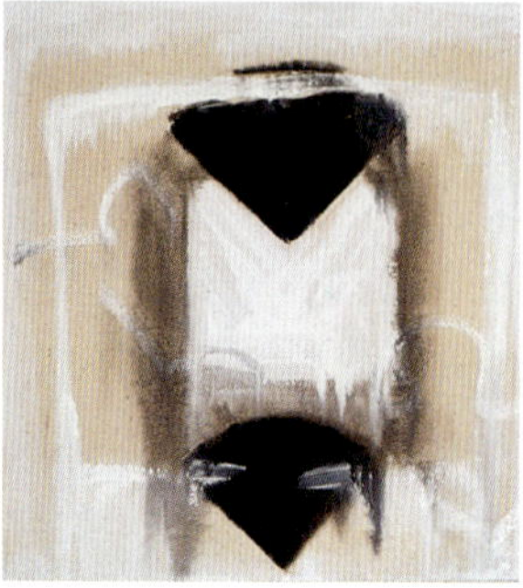

Chapter 7

An Alternative Paradigm: Developing an Aesthetic for the 1990s

Left:
Denise Green, *Hood*, 1992. Oil on canvas, 202 x 197 cm. Photograph: Nicholas Walster.

Centre:
Denise Green, *Scallywag*, 1992. Oil on canvas 35 x 35 cm. Collection: Art Galleries Schubert. Photograph: Nicholas Walster.

Right:
Denise Green, *Two Vessels*, 1992. Oil on canvas, 35 x 35 cm. Collection: Art Galleries Schubert. Photograph: Nicholas Walster.

The early 1990s was a turning point in both my work and my career. Since there was a severe economic recession in New York City at that time, it seemed pointless to expect major galleries to actively shape an artist's career. I therefore took the deliberate and strategic decision to attempt to have my work recognized in Europe. This meant learning to function as a painter in a European context and to write and speak reflectively about my art and my experience as an artist. My long-term goal was to ensure that my work would become the subject of museum shows and receive wider critical attention.

Writing about art made me aware, for the first time perhaps, that I was influenced by two traditions, not only the modernist tradition of the West, but also Asian and Aboriginal modes of thinking. It helped me become aware that the different cultural elements in my work fitted together like a mosaic. Today, we experience the phenomenon of artists who have migrated from one country to another and who carry the world of their origins within themselves while adapting to their new cultures. Their art works present different modes of thinking and configurations of the self. They differ from artists who have grown up and stayed in the same place and who are influenced by just one culture.

There was certainly a practical aspect that motivated my decision to go toward

Europe. But, in writing about my art, I began to realize more fully how painters had functioned in the New York art world since the 1950s. My experience in the classroom with Mark Rothko in 1969 is a good illustration. Although he was extremely articulate and cultivated, Rothko never explained or talked about his own paintings. In a text that appeared in *The Tiger's Eye* in 1947 he stated that painting lives by 'companionship'.[1] Implicit in this idea was the attitude expressed in a joint letter written by Rothko and Adolph Gottlieb,[2] which was that the viewer must be moved by looking at a painting and that understanding the painting is not dependent on explanation. They contended that the work must speak for itself, using the language of colour and shape without personal reference.

Before the 1950s Rothko's position had been different. Highly lucid about his aesthetic beliefs, he had expressed his ideas during an important stage of development leading to the signature style. Between 1943 and 1949 he wrote statements which formed a virtual manifesto for Abstract Expressionism and which were crucial for critics and art historians in their deciphering of the new language of abstraction. I had read these statements in the 1949 edition of *The Tiger's Eye*, which describe the painter's progress toward clarification. What hindered the clarification of ideas for Rothko were factors such as memory, history and geography.

Rothko's tendency towards silence meshed with Clement Greenberg's formalist approach and founded a critical paradigm still relevant today. It became the norm in America that painters did not offer explanations for their work. Living in such an atmosphere, I didn't explain or write about my work until I became involved in Europe where I had to become more articulate. This offered a broadening of the American tradition where one only painted, but did not speak of one's work.

It was also in 1991 that a startling change took place in the work itself. Suddenly colour dropped out and I began painting exclusively in black and white. When these new works were shown in 1992, and I saw them in the gallery, they revealed a deeper level of meaning than I had suspected. No one else could write about this accord between the work and my inner experience, and I wanted these paintings to be understood not only in formal, but also in more personal terms. Luckily my editor in Paris encouraged me to speak about the sudden changes in my work. Over the next ten years of writing I came to realize that even if these paintings used an abstract vocabulary they were drawing on a bank of stored images, both personal and cultural,

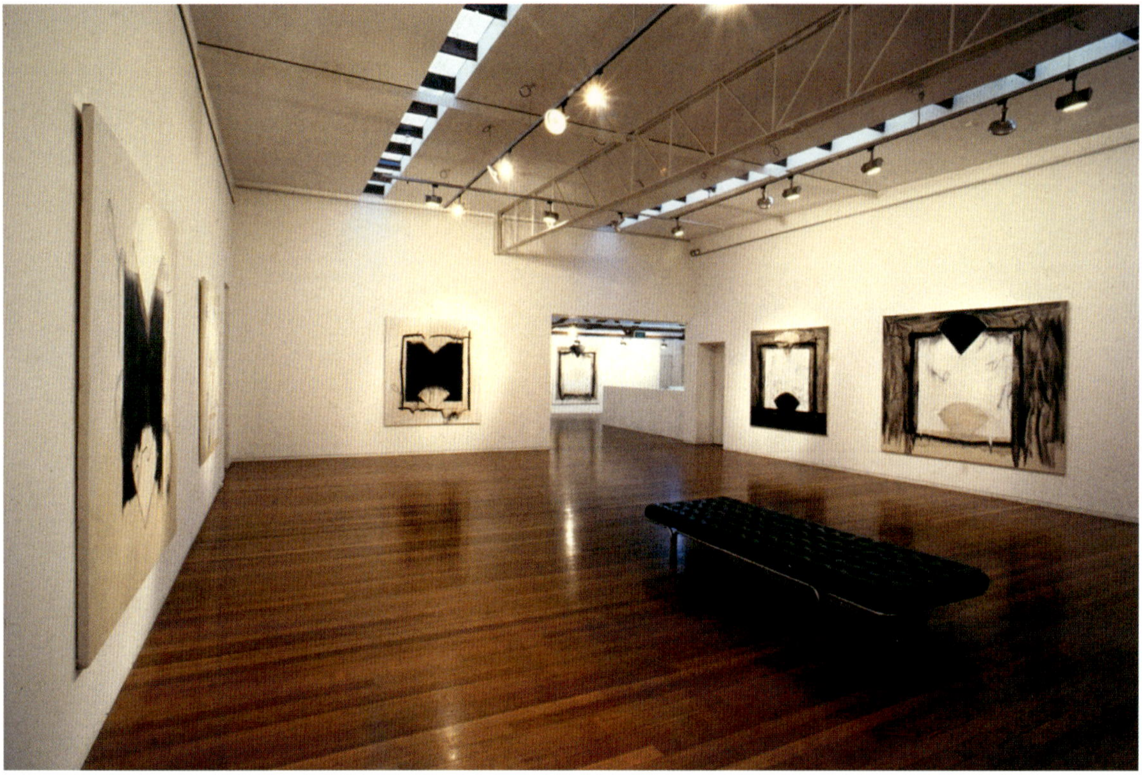

Denise Green,
Installation view of
Roslyn Oxley Gallery
exhibition, 1992, Sydney.

which told the story of my life. Understanding my own story and its artistic progress helped my work to develop. I gained this understanding through writing and thereby telling my story to myself.

When a viewer looks at a work of art it is essential that they bring to it their own experience and understanding – and this can vary considerably from one viewer to another. Because the turn in my work was so dramatic, I need to explain the motivation that led to these changes. However it does not mean that this body of work should only be understood in this way. I am privileged to have an understanding of some of my creative processes, but ultimately the work has to stand on its own.

Within one day I suddenly began painting only in black and white! While working on a group of large canvases, I also found another way of mixing paint which allowed for some additional subtle changes. Curiously, behind the choices concerning colour, composition and the handling of the paint was a great deal of emotional energy. In contrast to the 1980s, when each painting had a different arrangement of geometric elements, now a symmetrical composition became the consistent feature. Two fan-like shapes, balanced in relationship to a square, asserted themselves. The square was in the center and the two quadrants, by sitting on their points, became stable in relationship to each other and the square.

But the most important change had to do with how the choice and use of materials allowed for a greater integration of the pictorial space. Instead of drawing directly on the canvas with paint sticks, I worked in a totally different way. Unlike the traditional way of mixing oil paint with the medium on the palette, I first spread the medium over the whole canvas and then added black oil paint to it.[3] The paint dissolved into the medium and took on a life of its own, by both fitting into the composition and defying any set lines or boundaries. In some areas it had a dense black presence and in others it was more diluted and made drips and runs in subtleties of gray. Sometimes the medium was visible as a transparent layer, allowing the natural shade of the canvas to function as a colour. This unusual way of using the medium dissolved edges and softened the shapes.

Only in retrospect did it occur to me that the change had been stimulated by feelings of grief for my father, who had died in Australia in 1969. I was in art school in France at that time, and had not grieved for him. But as the work began to change dramatically, thoughts of my father entered my conscious mind. I now realize this new

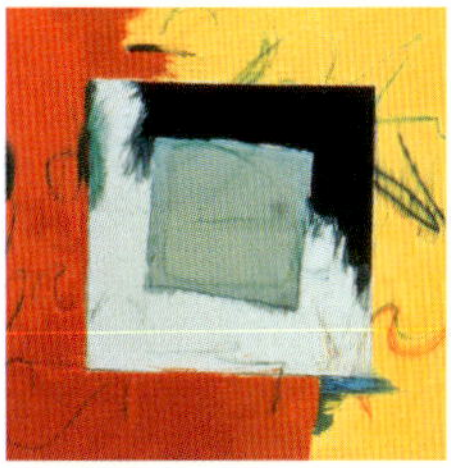

Denise Green, *Hawthorne*, 1986. Oil and wax on canvas, 183 x 183 cm. Collection: Art Gallery of New South Wales, Sydney. Photograph: Nicholas Walster.

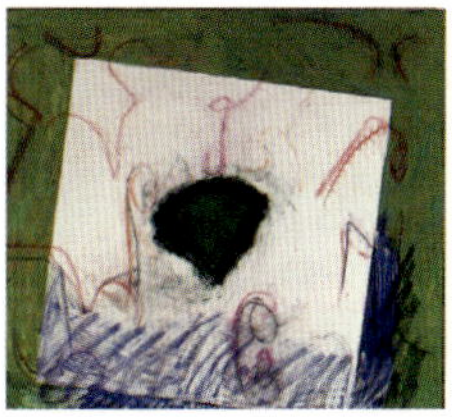

Denise Green, *The Great Escape*, 1987. Oil and paintstick on canvas, 173 x 178 cm. Photograph: Nicholas Walster.

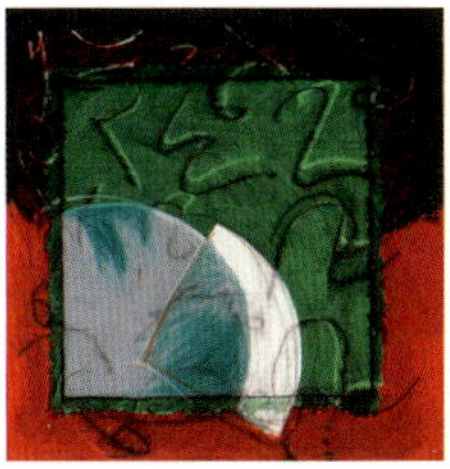

Denise Green, *Duane Triangle*, 1966. Paint stick and acrylic on canvas, 183 x 183 cm. Collection Michael Rayner, Brisbane. Photograph: Nicholas Walster.

development was the outcome of unconscious processes. The shift happened as I became more in touch with a repressed emotional experience that occurred twenty years earlier, and which was still an unconscious force in my life.

Since this change in my work I have gained a better understanding of it, largely due to reading an essay by Alan Roland, *Imagery and Symbolic Expression in Dreams and Art*.[4] Roland observes that imagery in art can encompass simultaneously both an artistic vision and internalized experiences of early family relationships. This is especially true when the art work has emotional power. The imaginative vision makes a statement of what the work is as art, but the emotional power draws on early experiences within the psyche dating back, perhaps, to childhood.

Roland goes on to explain that imagery in dreams can by-pass defense systems. Imagery in art can also by-pass these defences, especially when it relates to forbidden or repressed emotions.[5] When an artist works in a non-objective or abstract way, these emotionally charged inner experiences are expressed through colour, form and structure. As a consequence, an artist may not realize what motivates the work. In my family grieving was forbidden, yet in painting, through a change in colour and a different way of using the medium, I by-passed the veto and expressed the grief that had been repressed.

I am not commenting here on what the work looks like, but more on the creative processes that are involved in its production. Only the artist can talk about this.
As a result of the profound change in my work, in February 1994 I published an article in the French journal *Art Press*, on the subject of 'Painterly Thought and the Unconscious'. Commentators like Rob Storr responded to the article by claiming that painting conveying the artist's inner state through covering and hiding was related to the tendencies of the 1950s. I interpreted this as a reference to Twombly, whose paintings are linked to the tradition of Abstract Expressionism. Twombly's surfaces speak of smeared effacement. Curators say that his work is distinctive because it conveys a sense of life energy. They add that the overlaid lines and abstract scribblings in his work carry the burden of content. In his thoughtful consideration of the work, Varnadoe observed that, '. . . from the strokes and casual incidents of paint arises the work's authenticity, as a model of experience in process'.[6] These interpretations may be valid, but they leave the issue of the exploration of the creative impulses in Twombly's work unaddressed. Curators obviously are not able to consider

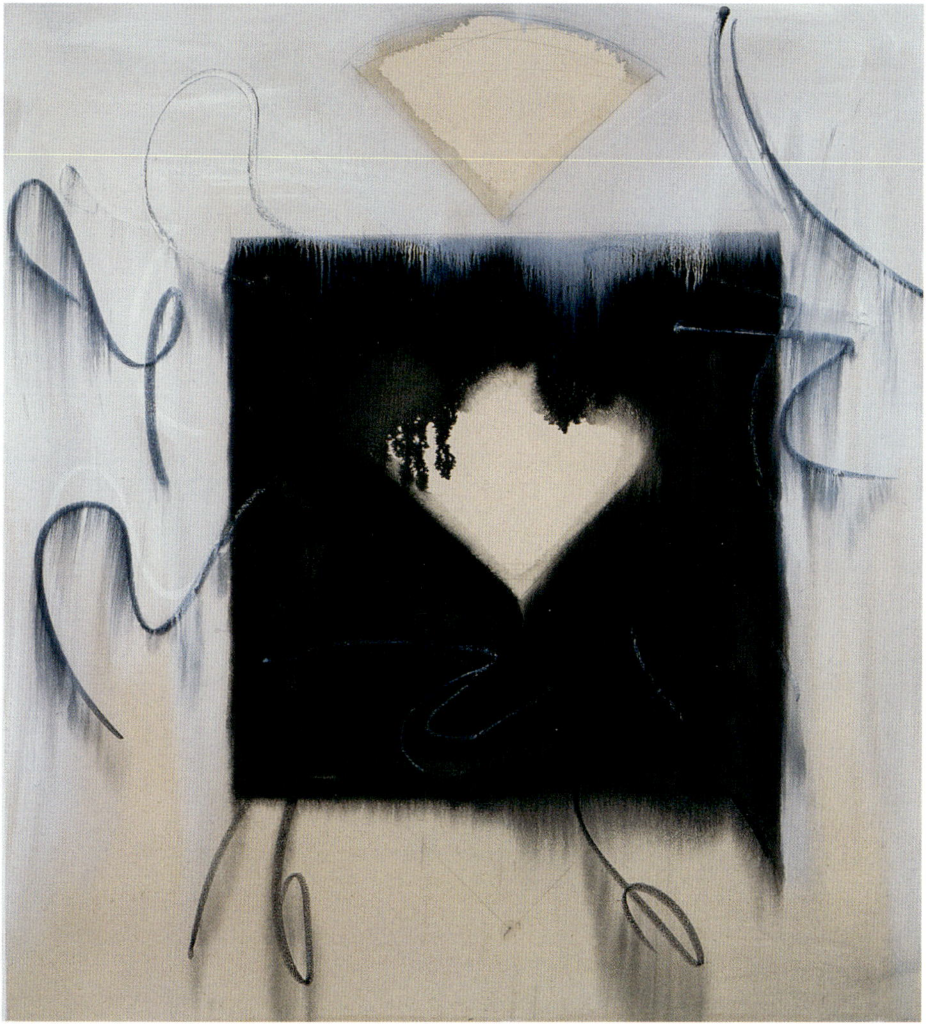

the emotions and state of mind that inform the work. Only the artist can elaborate upon those factors.

In my work I would prefer that the understanding of the creative processes be related to a monistic framework into which metonymic thinking is intrinsically connected. As I have discussed in earlier chapters, monism is an Eastern philosophical tradition that is fundamentally different from Western dualism. It emphasizes the

Denise Green, *Is That a Gun*, 1992. Oil on canvas, 122 x 122 cm. Collection: Anthony Pratt.

continuum between self and other and mind and body, in contrast to the Cartesian dualisms of Western thought. Within the monistic framework there is a continuity and continuum between the art work and the artist. Thus the statue of Uma, for instance, is a partial manifestation of the Goddess, and not a symbolic depiction of her.

The way this continuum is experienced is through metonymic thinking. When an artist creates metonymically, the art work is a seamless extension of the artist's state of mind. In describing my paintings from an Eastern perspective, I would consider them to be a partial manifestation of myself. The works that grew out of feelings of loss and absence do not symbolically depict those emotions, rather they are a direct portrayal of them. The metonymic process allows me to bring out many different aspects of my inner life, including those disavowed feelings that can only be expressed through paintings that convey this emotional state. However, I have no idea of what is being conveyed at the time that I am painting. It is only some time afterwards that I recognize what aspects of my inner life are in the painting.

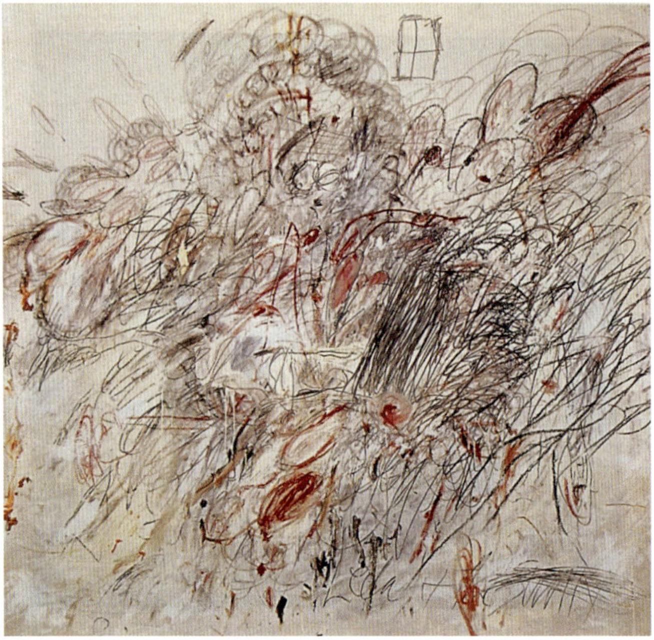

Cy Twombly, *Leda and the Swan*, 1962. Oil, pencil and crayon on canvas, 135 x 150 cm. Courtesy of the Artist.

Notes

1 'The Ides of Art: The Attitudes of 10 Artists on their Art and Contemporaneousness'. *The Tiger's Eye # 2* (December 1947), p. 44. *The Tiger's Eye* was a highly influential, quarterly art journal that first appeared in the fall of 1947.

2 [Letter]. In Edward Alden Jewell, 'The Realm of Art: A New Platform and Other Matters: "Globalism Pops into View"', *New York Times*, June 13, 1943, p. 9. (With Adolph Gottlieb and probably with the collaboration of Barnett Newman.)

3 The medium is a mixture of turpentine, stand oil and damar varnish in varying proportions, which is usually added to the oil paint on the palette.

4 Alan Roland, 1972. *Imagery and Symbolic Expression in Dreams and Art*, International Journal of Psychoanalysis, 53, 531, New York.

5 Alan Roland, 1981. 'Imagery and the Self in Artistic Creativity and Psychoanalytic Literary Criticism'. In this later essay, Roland actually formulates how imagery by-passes defences. He says 'when artists use imagery as a major aesthetic means of conveying abstract social meanings reinforced by the personal meanings, they by and large by-pass their own defensive structure. Imagery is therefore a window to the unconscious, even when used for aesthetic purposes. But, because imagery by-passes defences, the artist far more than others is able to tap his or her own unconscious, but essentially in the service of the artistic endeavor, and usually without any great increase in self awareness'. *The Psychoanalytic Review*, vol 68, No. 3, Fall 1981.

6 Kirk Varnedoe, 'Inscriptions in Arcadia' in *Cy Twombly: A Retrospective*, Museum of Modern Art, New York, 1995.

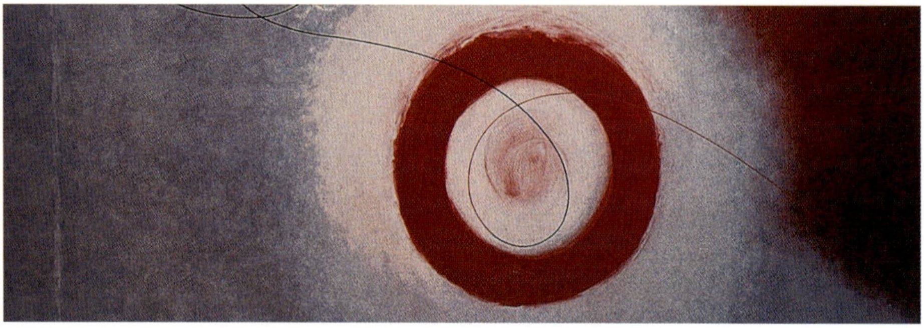

Dorothea Rockburne, *C*, $C^2 + C$ *and* $(C^2 + C)^2 + C$, 1993. Wall installation, (detail), Lascaux Acuacryl on gesso prepared surface. © 2005 Dorothea Rockburne/Artists' Rights Society (ARS), New York.

Chapter 8

Painterly Thought and the Unconscious:

Interviews with Alex Katz, Frank Stella, Dorothea Rockburne and Barry Le Va

Artists can be inspired in many ways. Sometimes it is the spectacle of a foreign place, for instance the effect Morocco had on Matisse, or it can be the interaction with other works of art or past traditions such as Brice Marden's empathy with Tung Chi'i Ch'ang, the sixteenth-century Chinese painter and theorist. Sometimes it is through dialogue with other artists. Robert Wilson, for instance, finds collaboration with artists like David Byrne, Lucinda Childs, Heiner Muller and Isabelle Huppert to be inspiring.

There are also times when an artist's work changes suddenly, or radically, or subtly – and a radical shift in his or her familiar imagery occurs. Many artists are not consciously aware of the reasons for such occurrences. Some changes are intuitive, others deliberate and calculated, still others are suppressed. Some artists will destroy drawings and paintings that show a sudden change in the direction of their work for fear that it would interfere with their career.

On 4 July 1991 I painted a series of nine small canvases which were influenced by the departure of a friend. As I continued working, my usual rainbow palette gradually disappeared until what remained was black and white. When other artists who are colourists, such as Matisse or Picasso, shift to black and white, it can be to clarify the spatial relationships within the image through an emphasis on drawing. When my work made the same shift, as I have explained in the previous chapter, a whole new range of emotional expression was unleashed. I did not need to clarify the spatial structure of my paintings by using black and white, rather I achieved a more cohesive formal structure, which integrated all the old and new elements with the exception of colour.

As I have mentioned previously, my work was being stimulated by disavowed emotions surrounding my father's death. I had not grieved for him when he died in 1969. I then realized that the shift in my work was based on the integration of an emotional experience which had occurred twenty years earlier and which, as I have explained, was still an unconscious force in my life.

This experience made me aware that changes in my work can be connected to feelings of which I am not totally aware, or that I might even deny at the time. The insight I gained from this experience was that the emotional power of a painting often comes from sources of which the artist is not always fully aware. What matters is to have access to an image, or emotion – and then to be able to use it effectively. Even though the meaning may remain hidden, the work can still communicate powerfully to a viewer.

The experience surrounding the sudden and startling change in my work formed the genesis for an article that appeared in 1994 in *Art Press* under the title 'Painterly Thought and the Unconscious'. I became curious to know if other artists had experienced similar radical changes in their work and where such occurrences had

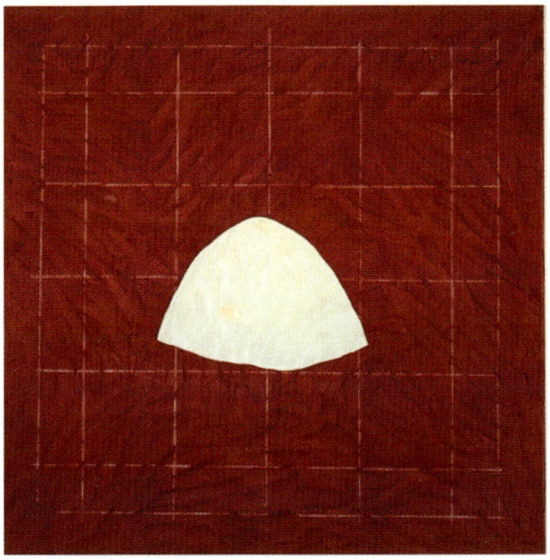

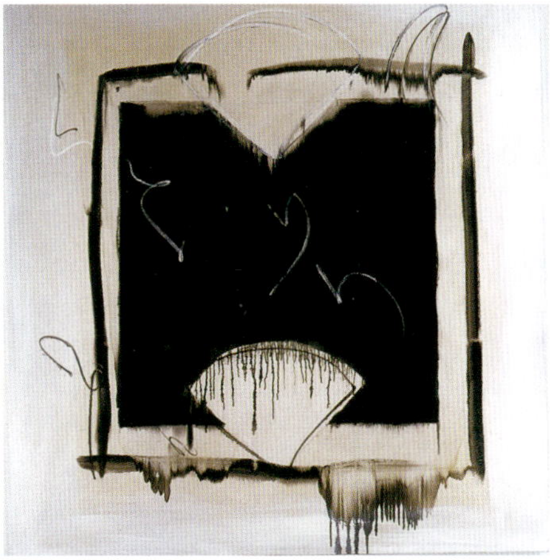

Left:
Denise Green, *The Longhouse*, 1977. Oil on canvas, 150 x 150 cm. Collection: Art Gallery of Western Australia, Perth Photograph: Nicholas Walster.

Right:
Denise Green, *Cinderella-What?*, 1992. Oil on canvas, 172 x 182 cm. Photograph: Nicholas Walster.

taken them. I questioned several New York artists about how they perceived those moments when their art seemed to take a spectacular new turn, when forms sprang up in the studio that took them by surprise. These were occasions when artists saw aspects of themselves they had never seen before and, without completely understanding them, did not block what was happening and let the work lead them forward. Artists may recognize a continuity running throughout their formal thought, but there are times when such thought allows for leaps, intuitions and premonitions after long intervals and a long way outside any idea of linear evolution. In my discussions with the following artists I was not concerned with their finished art works. Instead I was aiming to understand their creative processes. The artists are: Alex Katz, Frank Stella, Dorothea Rockburne and Barry Le Va. The following interviews, which were conducted in 1993, represent the responses I received from them.

Alex Katz

DG: In retrospect, what drew you to the scene that is depicted in *Wet Evening*?

AK: I just kept looking at it. It was about 9.30 at night and it was a wet evening. It was a click, an illumination. After that I had to bear responsibility for what I had to do. The change was that it turned out to be an eleven foot painting. I did sketches and then took a small panel. It was then a question of how big the paintings had to be. It took very little painting.

DG: Was there a series of earlier, related paintings?

AK: I had been doing black backgrounds from that same view for seven years. But this was the first time it became the whole painting. So it had a history. It didn't just appear, but it was markedly different.

DG: Was there then a series of later related paintings?

AK: I did *Wet Evening* and I couldn't figure out how to follow it. It was itself. To make ten more eleven foot paintings with the same subject matter would be a waste of time. It took a while to go to *Night II*, even though it would be a logical step away. But *Night II* had something for me to follow, to really extend. The values were clear, and I wanted my painting to look like that. It set a direction. It pointed the way I wanted to go for another ten years. But the series of works didn't come out at once. There were three month intervals. And other things were going on.

Black Brook came out of those paintings. It began to deal with the *effect* of what you see, rather than *what* you see. *Black Brook* is painted just like I paint the sketches. It's a very direct, disciplined, gestural way of painting. I think it relates to oriental brush painting as well as to abstract painting. I couldn't have accepted that before painting *Wet Evening*. That's what I mean, the *Black Brook* series are more abstract landscape paintings than I had done before.

DG: Part of my objective is to examine how the unconscious emerges when there's any kind of intuitive shift in the work.

Alex Katz, *Wet Evening*, 1987. Oil on canvas, 332 x 332 cm. © Alex Katz/Licensed by VAGA, New York, New York.

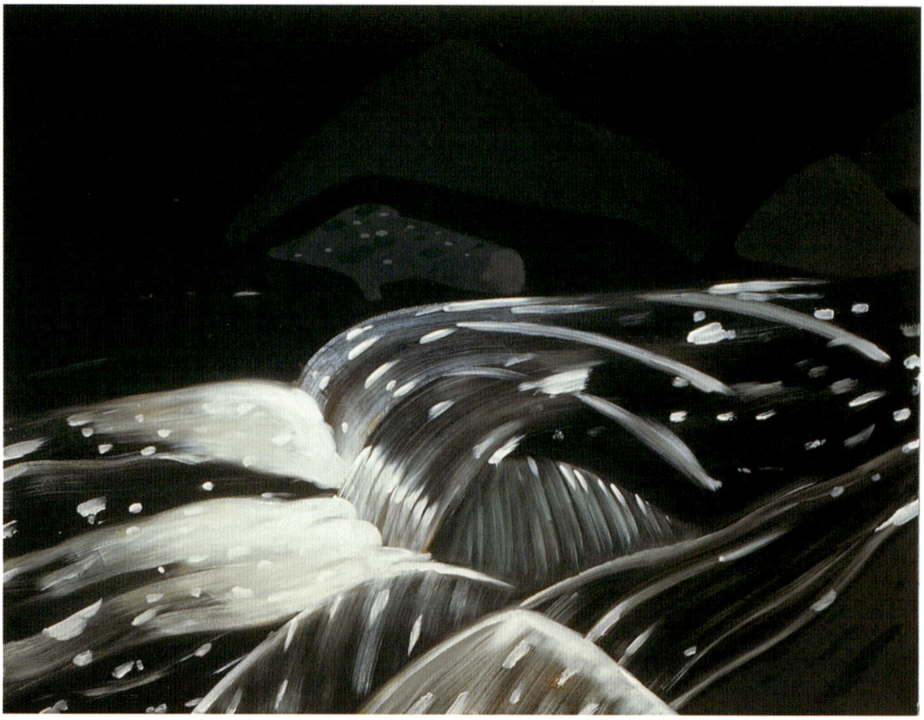

AK: In painting you discipline your unconscious for when you want it to open up and when you want it to close down. One of the great experiences as a painter is to open the unconscious up and let it fly. It's the internal rhythms and music of the artist that really gives energy and strength to the paintings. Rhythms that come from inside dictate what the painting will look like. These are much more important than anything else.

DG: In terms of your life outside of painting, was there something that may have been suppressed earlier and that came out around the time that you painted *Wet Evening*?

Alex Katz, *Black Brook 4*, 1990. Oil on canvas, 182.88 x 243.84 cm. © Alex Katz/Licensed by VAGA, New York, New York.

AK: I think the development of my ego and ambition, and restlessness, are what make me want to do something I haven't already done. Then, I don't feel I'm static. I think it is like an internal rage that I don't have much control over. It is an assertion of ego or something like it, and it is also a desire not to be bored in the studio. I don't want to be bored like a grand master making masterpieces. That's my idea of dying.

DG: How does the rage tie into that?

AK: The rage is the drive.

DG: How come it happened in the last ten years?

AK: I think it was always happening.

DG: Did something take place around 1986?

AK: I had a retrospective. I decided when you have a retrospective you've got to go back and start all over and do something you haven't done before. Otherwise you end up like many painters – just painting worse pictures than you painted earlier. Since then I've done some of the best pictures of my life. I did all those multiple figure paintings. I liked them and I thought they were a big step. I don't know if I've done anything better than *Luna Park* or *The Black Dress* from 1960, but the black *Night II* paintings are more cohesive. I'm more skilful. I can do more things more easily now. I have the brains not to make some mistakes.

DG: Do feelings emerge from your paintings that surprise you?

AK: Actually I expect other people to tell me what I have painted. I know what I'm trying to do, and the technical aspect of what I am doing, but a big part of the painting, if it's any good, comes from another part of your person. You create a process that will engage your whole being and release something. When I started out, I had no idea my paintings would seem 'Oriental', or calm. I thought they were very lively. In one of my first reviews, Frank O'Hara said the paintings had an Oriental calm. I was shocked at that, but I guess he was right.

DG: What does that mean to you, Oriental calm?

AK: That's part of my personality that I couldn't see. It is a bit like a person's handwriting.

DG: Just as this Oriental calm has emerged in your painting, is it also in your life?

AK: My whole life is absorbed by my painting. My life is fairly static. I've been in the same studio for twenty-two years. I don't like to move things around. I don't need a lot of excitement. I keep it as dull as I can. I need that kind of quiet.

DG: That's the parallel I would make. There is a quality of calm, something more meditative and inwardly directed that one senses in your work and your life as you live it from day to day.

AK: I think that's true. If you're bored in your studio, it's your own fault. I like the idea of being alone in the studio.

There were two issues that struck me in this interview as being revealing about Katz's creative process. I was especially intrigued by his reference to the use of the unconscious. There are different ways of using the unconscious, and Katz is using his to refer to things that are out of mind, but not necessarily repressed.

He says, 'It's the internal rhythms and music of the artist that really gives energy and strength to the painting. Rhythms that come from inside dictate what the painting looks like'. It seems to me that Katz is constantly trying to access a deeper part of himself. At other times, when he wants to resolve technical issues, he is less involved with this.

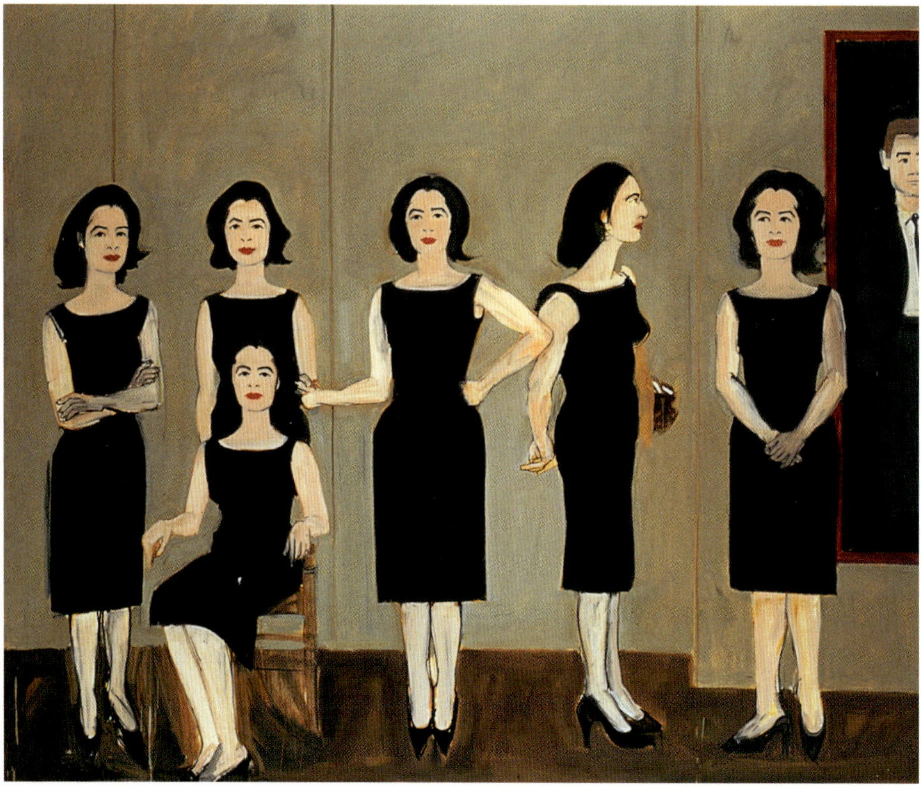

Alex Katz, *The Black Dress*, 1960. Oil on canvas, 181.6 x 212.1 cm. © Alex Katz/Licensed by VAGA, New York, New York.

Katz made a second important point when he emphasized how he does not want to be bored in the studio. This is his idea of dying.

So, it is crucial for Katz to keep himself open to what is inside. He hates repetition and is constantly opening himself up to something new. He is always pushing to do something different.

Frank Stella

DG: Does it ever happen that an intuitive shift emerges in your work, when you see something new that you haven't seen before? Has that ever happened to you, or would you say that your work represents a more even progression?

FS: No, it's an opportunistic process. I guess the difference is in the way you perceive the idea. When you have intuitive thoughts you often jot them down, and then they are not acted upon until quite a bit later. That's just a fact of life. While I was making the stripe paintings I was also working on a group of ideas for what would become the more eccentric polygon paintings. I made millions of little notations and drawings based on a different idea from that behind the paintings on which I was working at the time.

[At this point I told Stella the story about my father, and how a shift in my work was related to feelings that I had not been aware of at the time. I asked if anything similar had happened to him.]

FS: I suppose it has, but I have managed to stay out of touch with my unconscious. I go from one thing to another and I don't spend much time worrying about where it came from … I think it's an interesting idea that there may be such reasons for a shift. But I find it equally interesting that some things just appear to be finished at a certain stage. You can start to get tired of them, and then they really end. So, as an artist, you accept the fact that they're going to end and you start to look for something else. That's a problem for a lot of people because they say, 'I found a part of myself that's really me, now why am I going to abandon that?'. I think the 'me' is in the process, rather than in what you actually do.

DG: When you say you start to look for something else, what kinds of things are you referring to?

FS: I notice things on the outside that are very different from what I'm doing.

I also notice things in the work that I feel are hopeless. Firstly, some things are going to end; and secondly, that some things that are good are not being developed. In order to develop those good ideas that are there, I have to take them out of that context and find a new place to put them so that they can continue to grow. It is like having a grove of trees and, as if by accident, in the middle of your pine grove there's a beautiful little oak tree starting its life. You know that if you leave it there, the pines are going to dominate and it won't survive. So you have to take it out of context and put it some place else and see how it will do … .

It has happened a couple of times. While working on the shaped strip paintings, the idea of shaping and forming the surfaces, making a kind of image formed by the shapes themselves that made the exterior image happen, was OK. But the idea was good enough to go on and be used in other ways.
The protractor paintings and the eccentric polygon paintings were variations on these ideas, but they had to be taken out of the context of the repetitiousness and the absolute symmetry of the stripe paintings. That was a change, and then other things that happened in the shaping of the new polygons and protractors. The idea was scrambled a little bit, but then found a new outlet in the Polish pictures with their same kind of shaping, but more conventional interior relationships. A lot of people said they looked like constructivism, which in some ways they did, but it was a new way of getting at it for me and it, in turn, led to something unexpected. Rather than looking like constructivist work, the work changed from a kind of layered and three-dimensional relief towards an opened metallic three-dimensional relief in works like *Brazilian*, *Exotic Birds* and *Indian Birds*. They represent quite a change, but they're all tightly related. They are all variations which move on from each other. Rather than being an intuitive process, when it works best, it is a process something like playing leapfrog in two directions.

DG: If the work jumps ahead of you and something unexpected or unplanned happens, do you find that the new idea can be incorporated in your work subsequently?

FS: Yes, I guess it can. I worked on the black paintings, and the idea was basically of using repetition and the pattern of stripes. Then I hit on an idea of shaping

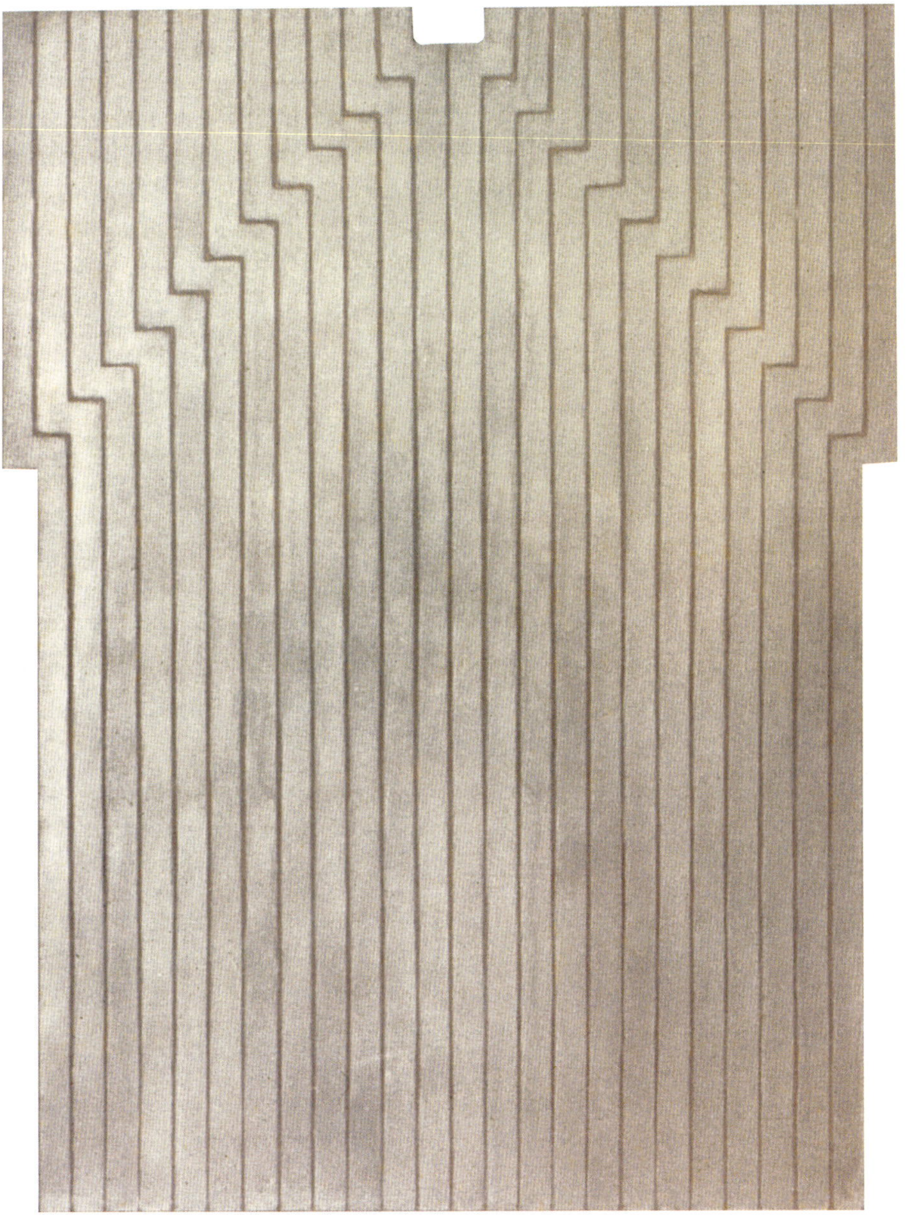

Frank Stella, *Luis Miguel Dominguin*, 1960. Aluminium paint on canvas, 230 x 177.5 cm.

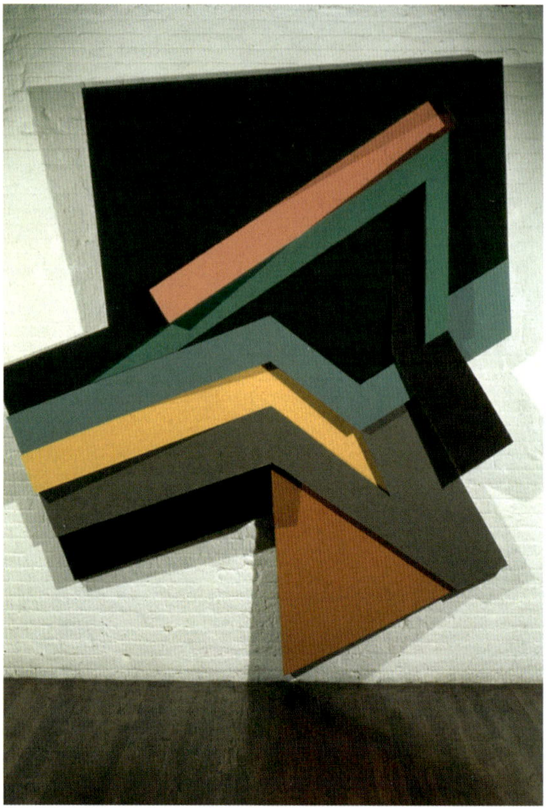

Frank Stella, *Lunna Wola III*, 1973. Relief collage, mixed media, 254 x 244 x 20 cm. © Frank Stella/Artists' Rights Society (ARS), New York.

that field, and that was the idea, shaping. But I had no idea that the consequences of notching or shaping a field would lead to the kind of thing that it did. Who would expect to go from something like *Dominguin [Luis Miquel Dominguin*, 1960], a simple aluminium painting with a few notches in it, to the *Moby Dick* pieces? The protractors were interesting because their idea showed up again later in *Moby Dick*, where the emphasis went from the straight line to the curve, and then to the circular pieces. The circular motif showed up in the curving and bending of the planes which occurred later in the eighties. It took a long time, and then it showed up again later.

DG: In retrospect, when you started working on the black paintings, was there anything specific that drew you to working like that?

FS: There was one thing. I don't know if it's abstract, or intuitive, or what. When I was working on the black painting, I was just making banded, repetitious paintings. The leap I made from there is that I started to look at the part that everyone talked about – which was the band or the stripe. I thought, am I just a designer? Am I just laying out a pattern, or am I really interested in the path that this mark travelled – which is more like traditional drawing or gesture? When I came to that, I started making simple abstract patterns. But I became very worried about the pattern, this band travelling from one edge to the other and basically spanning the surface. So then it began to take jogs and make turns. I made a lot of things that created patterns by jogging, by making turns. And that was it. Once I had that, I had created a different kind of field from the straightforward, symmetrically organized field. The problem was, in terms of design, that it gave me some left over stripes that didn't go anywhere. I showed that drawing to a friend who is a painter, Darby Bannard, and I said, 'Look, there is this terrific idea and it works, but these things are left over. I have these blocks and little holes in the middle and these pieces left over'. And he said, 'If you don't

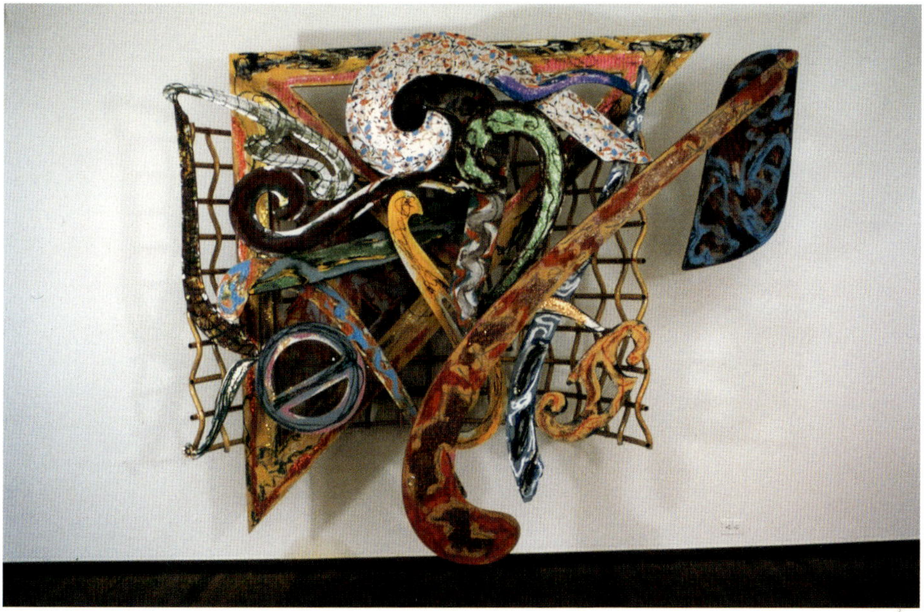

Frank Stella, *Jungli-Kowwa*, 1978. Mixed media, 215 x 254 x 96 cm. © Frank Stella/Artists' Rights Society (ARS), New York.

like them, why don't you just cut them away?'. That's what I did.

DG: Why were you so drawn to the energy and movement of those patterns? Did it connect to you personally?

FS: I don't know. There were Jasper's *Targets*, and Beckett was a big thing at that time. It was just an idea that was around and repetition was contrary to the way people were thinking about painting. When you're young, you like to be contrary. Everyone was saying how important every little expressive detail was that they did. And that's why it was great to be an artist. So I thought, I'll be an artist who does the same thing over and over again. It's not a very startling idea. It's a petulant adolescent reaction to a given situation, but in this case it became quite fruitful.

DG: Did you draw on any emotions for that, or things that you relate to yourself?

FS: You don't have to be Freud, as they say, to see in the black stripes that there was an adolescent depression at work. There was a pretty strong feeling. Alone in the city, it was a way of dealing with feelings. I think that is documented in the Baltimore catalogue by Brenda Richardson.

Stella's work is constantly changing with his unusual inventiveness in the use of formal elements. He is more interested in opening up new ideas than in repeating or consolidating ideas. For Stella, it's an internal cognitive process of developing ideas around painting.

In terms of his creative process, Stella talks about playing leapfrog in two directions to describe how his work progresses. My way of understanding this is that he goes back to his earlier work for ideas and then leapfrogs forward by using some of the previous elements in new contexts. The outcome is unpredictable and has led to a series of dramatic and surprising shifts. The leapfrogging plays a significant role in continuing his ability to shape new ideas.

Dorothea Rockburne

DG: Does it ever happen that an intuitive shift emerges in your work and you see something new that you haven't seen before?

DR: When I did *Neighborhood* (1972) I didn't really know what it was. It was based on set theory, but I couldn't understand the resulting wall drawing. I understood it emotionally, but not intellectually. It's not cubist or Byzantine space, and its geometry projects a different kind of space, too. Subsequently, I became very enticed with the Renaissance and took myself through the long journey of art history from Egypt through Italy and France. Then, in 1991, I was in Rome for four months and looked at a lot of Roman frescoes, certain aspects of which deal with time sequences. I started to study these mathematically, and that led into the work I am doing now. This new work is partly based on the Mandelbrot set [a mathematical operation that yields complex geometrical forms] from 1980 but I'm also dealing with the original concept that appeared in *Neighborhood.* There is something non-linear about making a work twenty-one years ago and having no idea what it was about. Just letting it be, recognising that it is different. I didn't know what it was, but I wanted to do it. Now I understand it.

DG: What was the surprise in the work?

DR: The surprise was not knowing what it was. Looking at it when it was finished, it seemed almost as if somebody else had thought it up and executed it.

DG: How did the change manifest itself?

DR: It projected a different kind of space. Now I realize it's the space of astrophysics, though I didn't know that then.

DG: You connected to this new kind of space emotionally, but did it relate to you personally?

DR: Yes, it seemed to be something that I visualized in my inner self and had to make. I had to see it realized in some way.

DG: It's curious how sometimes when shifts occur in your work, they connect to something going on within yourself. When something new happens in the work, it's almost like a moment of crisis.

DR: I don't find that. Usually I have a pretty good idea of what I want, even though I don't visualize it in fine detail. I just work until what is on the outside is the same thing that I'm visualizing. After doing all the set-theory work, that involved

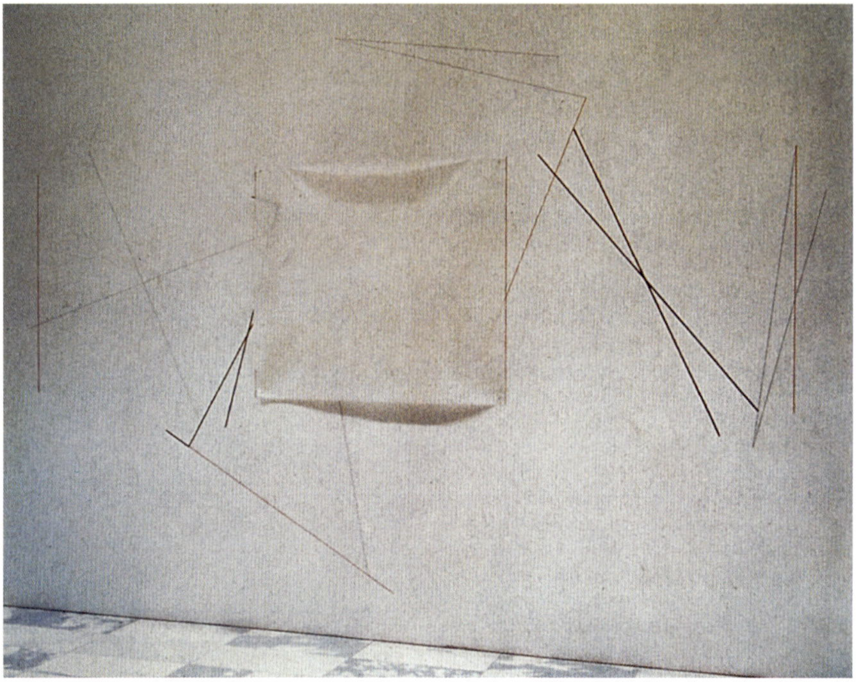

paper, boards, crude oil and other kinds of oil and grease, I remember I began to visualize this work, *Neighborhood*. I kept reading the equations for it over and over again, kept seeing it in my mind's eye, and it seemed very exciting.

DG: So it was a progression in your thinking?

DR: No, it was a leap. I based all the early work on set theory – paintings such as *Intersection, Disjunction* and *The Domain of the Variable* – which are beautiful, but quite understandable. But this work, *Neighborhood*, came seemingly out of nowhere. It's what I call 'horizontal growth proceeding from vertical growth'. There's all this horizontal thinking and then suddenly it goes bingo and, after a lot of work and struggle, there is this new thing, fully grown – and I've puzzled over it for twenty years. I've had two very unusual experiences in this way. *Neighborhood* was one of them. Another occurred when I was producing the *Pascal* paintings (1987-1988). Each painting was comprised of two or more separate canvases, painted completely and then layered. I did preliminary

Dorothea Rockburne, *Neighborhood*, 1973. Wall paint, pencil, coloured crayons, vellum. Collection: Museum of Modern Art, New York. © 2005 Dorothea Rockburne/Artists' Rights Society (ARS), New York.

studies for them in watercolour on vellum so that I could see through the layers. Then it came time to actually paint them in oil on canvas. I painted them quite separately, one from the other, because I wanted to work from another kind of internal source. I didn't want to think when I was painting. I just wanted to go on this other knowledge which I don't care to call intuition. However, while I was painting this particular area, something began to force me to paint it in a way that really surprised me. I was surprised because it was so far away from the preliminary watercolour. When I put the two shaped canvases together, the shadow that was cast by the six-inch stretcher bar onto the rear panel was real, whereas the shadow that was painted on the front panel was a painted illusion. To my surprise they worked together. The title of that painting is *Black and White* – even though I have used colour.

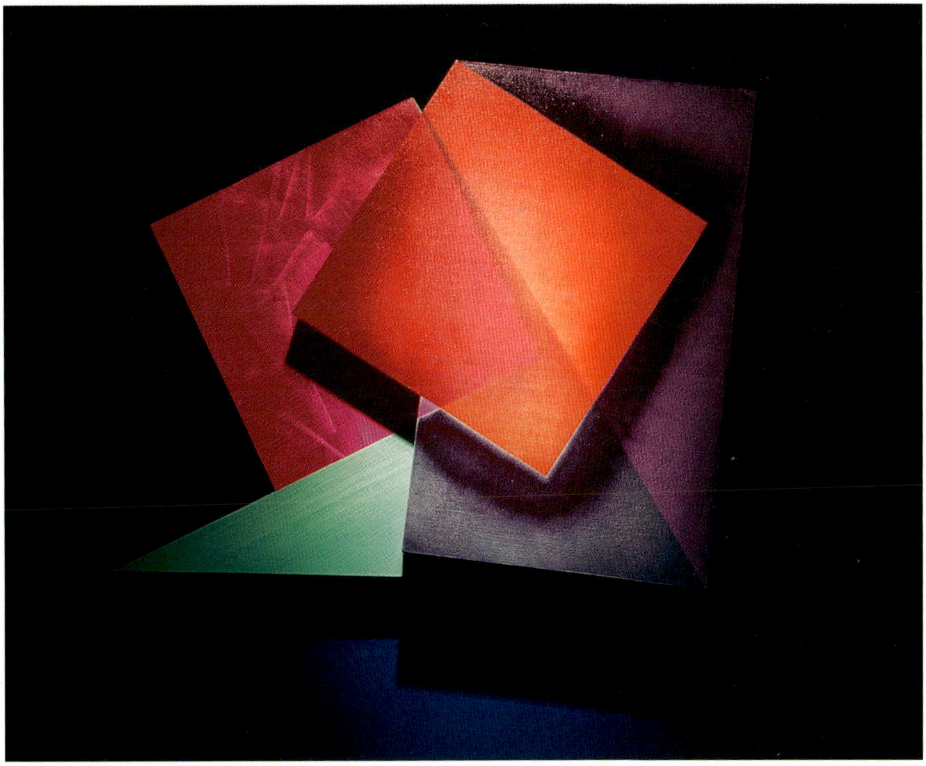

Dorothea Rockburne, *Black and White*, 1987. Oil on gessoed linen, 107.3 x 135.8 x 25.4 cm. © 2005 Dorothea Rockburne/Artists' Rights Society (ARS), New York.

DG: It is like a turning point when something like this happens.

DR: Absolutely. There are certain yardsticks in one's life and one's work. I could never have done the *Sony* piece (in 1991) without having done *Neighborhood*. I had to have that information in my bones, otherwise I wouldn't have been able to move forward.

DG: [I asked Rockburne if she had ever experienced the same discovery as I had when a shift in my work proved to be related to feelings for my father.]

DR: Not in the sense that you're talking about. I think that the reason I paint, or that I do whatever I do, is to deal with (I don't think of it as unconscious) subliminal knowledge. And I do think that one has knowledge about things that haven't occurred yet, and I try to work for those kinds of knowledges. For me, these are emotional truths. If I'm working with certain aspects of mathematics, they really serve as emotional truths in a way. For instance, if I'm very sad and I work, I tend to leave those emotions at the door and I work on what I'm thinking about, although my feelings are always there and ever present. It's not a cold process.

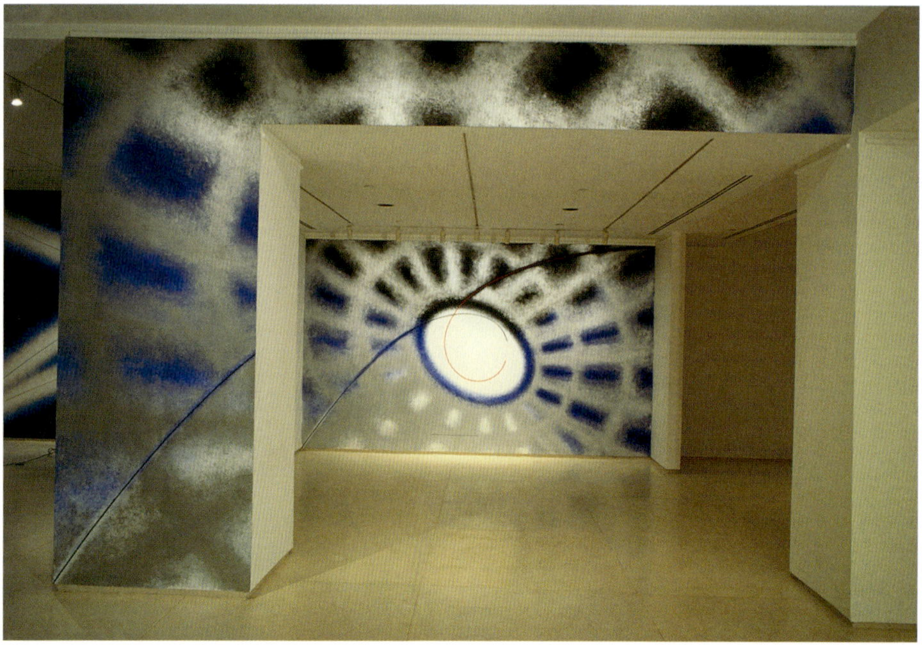

Dorothea Rockburne, *First Day*, 1993. Wall installation of Lascaux Acuacryl on gessoed surface. © 2005 Dorothea Rockburne/Artists' Rights Society (ARS), New York.

Yet in a true sense I'm always working on the next idea.

DG: Is it possible to be explicit about how subliminal knowledge has influenced the realization of your work?

DR: It is what I call developed intuition. What I have found is that when I learn something – when anybody learns something – while you are using it at the moment, it's right at the top of your brain. But, as you move on and are using newer information, the formerly learned information goes into a mental file and with time that file goes deeper into the drawer and becomes what I call subliminal information. It is trained intuition because the files begin to combine, all on their own accord.

DG: When you talk about *Neighborhood* you describe how it just came out and that now, twenty years later, you have it more in perspective. Is what you are doing now, in 1991, integrating the leap that took place then?

DR: Yes, but it's also in the *Pascal* paintings (from 1987-1988). In all of the paintings, I've been studying physics and light, and one of the problems in set theory is identity – I've been identifying things. I always title a painting before I do it, so I know what it is. And there's a lot of problems of identity – never making adjustments and never designing a work and working from another construct.

DG: So the new inspiration that has occurred in the last three years has incorporated the leap and the way that you got so far ahead of yourself in 1971. You have caught up with that now.

DR: It's not so much catching up as it is integrating it. It's an integration process.

In this interview I was caught completely by surprise at how different Rockburne is in her approach. Her changes are not fueled by unconscious emotions. She says she leaves her feelings at the door when she works, but her drawings and wall paintings embody emotion. Rockburne has a unique capacity for visualization. She has twice had a leap in her thinking and produced work that seemed to come out of nowhere. When this happens, she believes the work manifests a latent understanding of mathematical knowledge which she may come to comprehend cognitively many years later.

She described how, in 1973, she began to visualize equations for her wall drawing *Neighborhood*. This work, in which folded vellum, pencil and coloured lines re-configure the space for drawing itself, utilizes topology and was a step towards non-Euclidean geometry. She says of this work that it was like a Northern Star in her life. It guided her. She gradually gained a perspective on it, and only integrated the new ideas about space that evolved from it some fifteen years later.

Barry Le Va

DG: Has it ever happened that images or ideas have come into your work, and you develop these elements without knowing what they mean to you?

BLV: I can answer this in a number of ways. I may start with an inkling of an idea, without knowing where it is going to take me. I'll keep working until I find some reason for it to exist and also to judge its possibilities for making a work of art. It starts out sometimes with a drawing process, like jotting or doodling that leads me someplace – for example, how certain three dimensional forms will appear in space. Eventually, I'll try to figure out the subject matter, or it makes itself clear the more I work on it. Then I start the critical decision-making process, like what to include, or not. Once this becomes clear, I know exactly what I'm doing.

DG: Have the shifts in your work been deliberate? Or do they happen by accident?

BL: Both. A lot of times they are calculated just because I get bored. Or things happen as planned accidents. It's not that I work at only one thing at a time. For instance, if I'm doing a sculptural exhibition or a series of drawings, I start with one idea, and then let it sit. Maybe six months later I start with another and then combine the two. Eventually different ideas, thoughts and forms get filtered into the same material.

DG: What fuels the development in your work?

BL: My own personal excitement about discovering something.

DG: Are the emotions or ideas linked to some unconscious source?

BL: A number of the series I have tried to produce were possibly related to unconscious, or subconscious experiences that I have had. But I didn't know how to give them three-dimensional form. I was possibly too close to the situations provoking the thoughts. After four or five years I will have digested the experience, and the emotions will cease to exist.

DG: Recently there was a change in my work. The colour disappeared and I began painting in black and white. It was only after a year had passed that I realized how emotions in the work were connected to my father. This made me aware that changes can be connected to feelings that one is not aware of at the time.

BL: Most people thought the last group of sculptures I showed in New York (1992) was the most emotional work I had ever done. I would tend to agree with that, but I had pushed up the scale and the size. I made them monumental.

DG: Can you say anything more?

BL: The works were based on feelings associated with misunderstanding something. I tend to like my work to exist in the realm of slight confusion. Slight anxiety. Is it this, or is it that? This is why a lot of forms come from triple sources that I combine. It's like inventing an ideogram, that you don't read linearly. I know what it means, but a lot of people don't. Hopefully the formal issues – size, scale, process, material – will carry the emotion into the work.

DG: Can you give me an example when you say you understand what it means?

BL: In the last group of works, the forms were taken from templates such as you often have for architecture and other kinds of things. What you're seeing on the wall is looking down at a template. It may be a rectangle, but in its relationship to something else it is not just that, it is looking down at a table. And maybe the next form is looking down at a stool, or a chair. Since they're taken from templates, people will see these forms as geometric. Of course they are, but they are also a language in themselves. And when I see a rectangle in one position, and a round form, or a stool that you're looking down at, in another, I know exactly where the relationship comes from, because I have been in that position. It implies a position, maybe, of somebody sitting in a chair and at a table, talking across from me. That's how they sit. I think architecturally, in terms of floor plans, so where things are placed have definite meanings.

DG: I remember you did a piece in 1978 in which you had a breakthrough. It was titled, *A Continuance … (Accumulated Vision Blocked).*

BL: I blocked the process. So the spectator had to take in the negative as much as the positive.

DG: What happened after this work?

BL: I went as far as I could with that one thing, and after four or five years of developing it, the issues changed and the forms changed too.

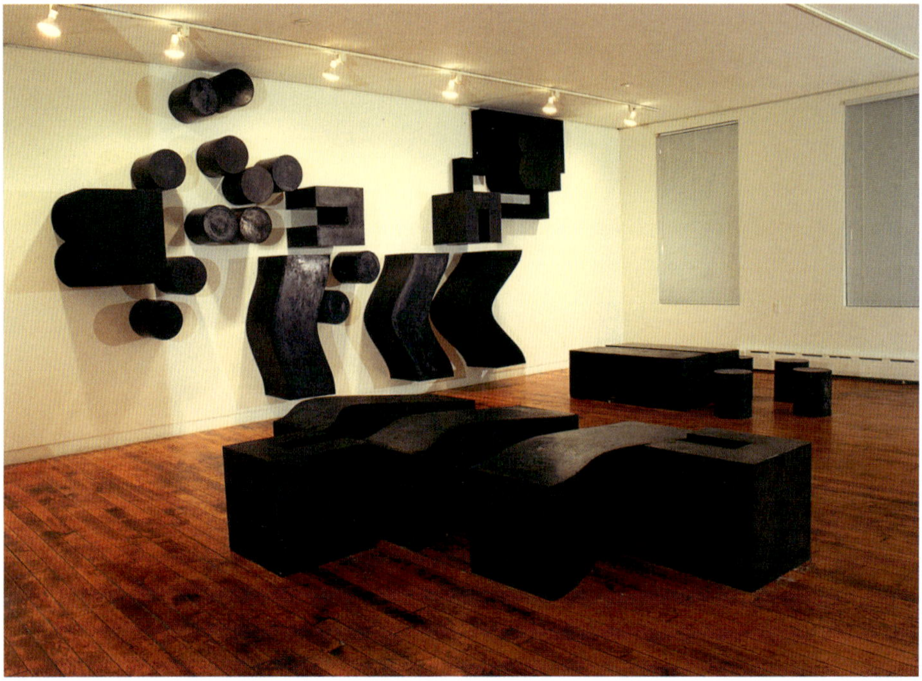

Barry Le Va, *Dissected Situations: Institutional Templates*, 1990-1991.
A. Spaces/Abbreviations.
B. Close-ups/Distances.
C. Observers/Participants.
Diagnostics – CBF with unknown vairable (10 observers). Cast black hydrastone and neoprene.
Dimensions variable.
Courtesy of the Artist.

The *Continuance* and *Blocked* works were kind of like using only one part of the body. It was as if by using your eye in a position, you had to project yourself outside in order to keep yourself inside, and thus sort out the piece. But it seemed to be stable. I guess you could say I was moving into a sculpture that would just crumble, subvert itself on its own, with a variety of elements that seemed to be totally unstable – like the aluminium balls that had no set positions. This idea also started from carrying out simple tasks.

DG: Do you try to pin down what is stimulating you?

BL: Not at the beginning. Then I am very open. I pin the idea down the more I play with it, and then the critical decision-making has to start. My drawings are like scripts. They are possibilities. They aren't absolute end results. In my thought processes I like to subvert. I could have a drawing here, and another there, and when it comes time to do the sculpture, I may have ten drawings. I'll take a section of this one, and that one. It's like calculated improvisation.

DG: What happened when the work evolved from installations with components on the floor and walls to scaled up three-dimensional objects?

BL: I got tired of ephemerality and improvisation – of not having made certain decisions made beforehand and having to think very fast during the installation. The early floor pieces were obviously subject to chance and process. Then I wanted things to be more calculated. So the investigation changed.

DG: You said earlier you were moving toward sculpture that started with simple tasks. And then a variety of things happened.

BL: I tend to investigate bodily functions, or situations in which I have been. These are situations that include the body, but the body is like a ghost. It is not in it. The forms have a relationship to a human activity, but I have taken the person out and left the furniture.

DG: You have also mentioned how there were psychological associations; and that you were digesting hospital experiences.

BL: Yes.

DG: You said a lot of the work was emotionally charged because it was based on personal experiences. And you referred to the geometric forms and how their scale also carries emotion into the work.

BL: Let me clarify the emotions underlying the work. I translate these real, physical

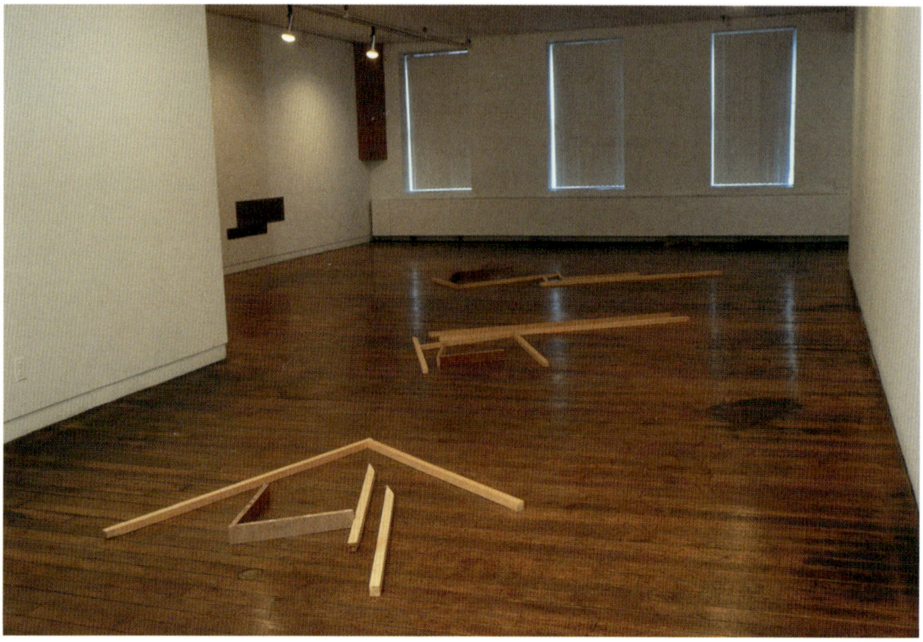

relationships that exist in space and that are the result of emotional situations – or possibly, even, unemotional situations. I spatially translate, almost verbatim, the arrangement of how things were. I filter the arrangement of furniture into geometric forms and you get a sense of something going on, but you cannot pin-point it. It becomes elusive. But none of these relationships are formal compositions. All the relationships are taken actually from real life and my own experience.

DG: And some that are anxious?

BL: Sure. And a lot of things are taken out of scale. For example, maybe somebody abbreviated something and I couldn't figure out what it meant. I would then combine this with a floor plan of something else, and would get those big linear forms.

Barry Le Va, Installation Sonnabend Gallery, New York, 1978. *... (Accumulated Vision-blocked).* Masonite and wood. Courtesy of the Artist.

DG: Would the abbreviation have a specific meaning for you?

BL: They did originally have very specific meanings. I referred earlier to how there are private languages, like in the medical profession, and if you do something like this [Le Va writes the letters CPE], the abbreviation has nothing to do with me, it just means chronic or cardiac pulmonary emphysema. But the public is not going to know what it means.

DG: Perhaps they don't need to.

BL: I don't really need to know what it means. But it's a language that confuses me. It makes me anxious. Because I might ask, what does that mean? And they'll say we're putting this down because of this and that. And I'll ask, is that what I have or is that the way it is, and they'll say no.

DG: So, you have access to the abbreviation and it is sufficient?

BL: I do research. Meaning that for the last group of sculptures, I had a book *Common Abbreviations in Clinical Medicine*. I can re-invent a form by using it on two levels. Something could look like a floor plan but, if you mentally scale it down, you can see it as an abbreviation. I like these double or triple meanings.

DG: As I mentioned earlier, what happened to me was that suddenly I got in touch with grieving emotions and they came out in my work. Even though at the time I wasn't sad or depressed, part of my inner reality was about those feelings. For three years I drew on those feelings as a source – for the choice of colour in my work, for example. To the extent that there are several levels of meaning in your work, does it interest you to identify some of the emotions?

BL: When you say grieving, mourning or depression, I can't work under those conditions. I may have felt these kinds of things, but I tend to work with a very calculated kind of distancing, by pulling things out that I remember. But it's very hard for me to deal with the notion of grieving or happiness in making a work. The outcome either has to be bewildering or confusing. Let's say at a certain time I could be bewildered, and the bewilderment causes anger. I don't know how to make angry sculpture, but I can control the elements in the space and make them bewildering, exactly from my own situation of what I'd witnessed. So I will go more for the notion of bewilderment than let's say anger or grief, because I don't know how to express those things.

DG: I see how your drawings and sculptures communicate on one level as abstract, yet they also connect to your inner reality and objectify it.

BL: Absolutely. I was going to go back to how you referred to a breakthrough in my work. It went from the accumulated pieces, things about positions and the 'blocked' series, and then I started to use what was inside of me as opposed to outer things. I started using real kinds of situations and experiences as opposed to just using the 'eye' or the 'ear'. I was trying to use all the inner things as opposed to the outer things. Now I'm trying to put them all together.

I can't say this was an emotional breakthrough because it was calculated. I can sit there and figure out what I have investigated. I've investigated certain processes – how the eye works processing location and position. Then I started using my own thought processes to figure out what I wanted to do. I started thinking that I had done all these other kinds of things to structure the work and asked myself why don't I just structure the work the way the thought processes go. It was just another part of my own body to investigate. To make something clearer about how one thinks, to make a work of art that's not necessarily about thinking, but the process of thinking. It was a breakthrough to go from certain bodily functions, processes and materials to an investigation of how my brain works.

In this interview Le Va is unusually capable of articulating his inner processes. His work lends itself to being interpreted metonymically. I find it fascinating that he can create drawings and installations using templates which reference his own interactions with people. He then conveys the charged emotion of these encounters through formal elements, such as size, scale, process and material.

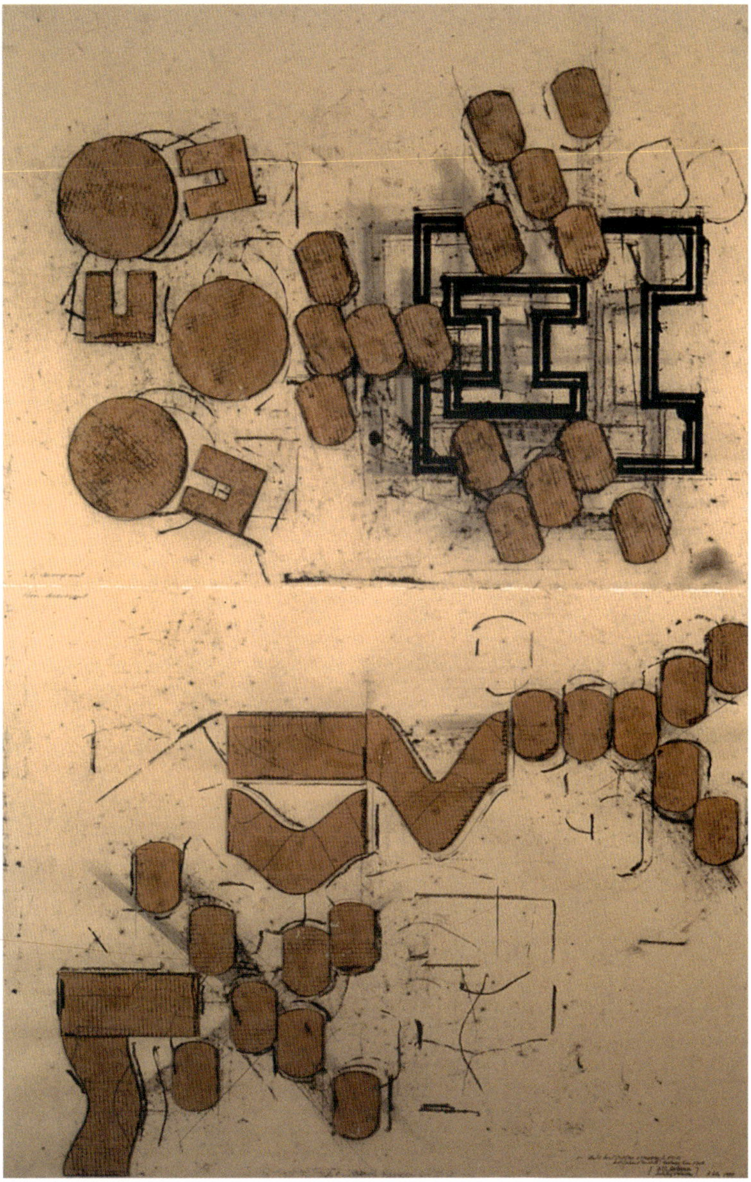

Barry Le Va, *Study for 1 Sculpture Occupying 2 Areas. Institutional Templates: Reading from Above*, 1990. NTL Conference Isolating Variables. Collage on paper, 151 x 384 cm. Courtesy of the Artist.

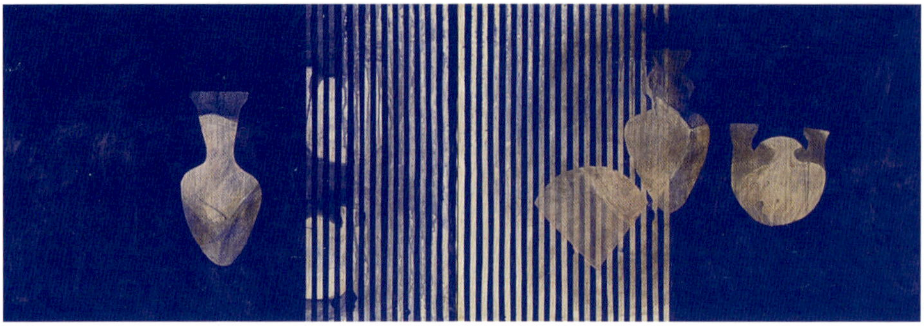

Denise Green, *Blue Re-Witnessing*, 2001. Acrylic on canvas, 112 x 316 cm. Courtesy Anthony Grant Inc., New York. Photograph: Nicholas Walster.

Chapter 9

Seeing the Attack : 11 September 2001

One: Seeing the Attack

I was in the studio the day of the attack. I got there early, having just returned from a vacation in Venice. A large two-panel canvas was leaning against the wall waiting to be started. My studio looks both north and west. The windows that face west have views to the south. About 8.45 am I heard police sirens and saw fire trucks heading down Varick Street. On Canal Street everyone had stopped walking. They were looking south toward Wall Street, gazing up at the sky. They looked shocked. I moved immediately to the windows at the back of the studio and saw the fire and the black gaping hole in the north tower of the World Trade Center. I opened the window and sat on the wide ledge outside, staring in disbelief at the spectacle. Black smoke poured out of the building, fire inching its way up the floors above the black hole.

I sat transfixed on the ledge outside my window. Then the second plane hit. I heard on the television in my studio that a plane had crashed into the Pentagon. I saw an image of Air Force One and realized that President Bush was a potential target. People were running over the footbridge that leads from Hudson Street. They were holding tissues over their faces to shield themselves from the smoke and fumes. Many people were crying. Suddenly, I noticed people on top of the buildings one block south of my studio. I kept looking at the towers, wondering how the fire could be contained, hypnotized by the intense orange glowing ominously within the steel frame of the tower. Small black objects were dropping from the upper area of the tower. I realized that people were falling. On the television, reporters were interviewing people trapped on the upper floors, who were saying they were calm and confident they would be rescued. I knew these people would not be rescued. I commented to a friend over the phone on how strongly built the towers were. Still standing despite the fire and damage, they seemed indestructible. At that moment, with a slow grace, one of the towers was engulfed in an enormous cloud and started sinking. I screamed.

Crowds of people were running up Varick Street. I sat in front of the television. For three hours I watched and wondered what to do. I thought about leaving. I thought about calling someone, but I stayed transfixed, just looking at images on the screen and listening to reporters. After several hours I knew I wanted to be in front of my canvas. I had already spread colour powder pigment over the surface and now I started putting anything down on the canvas. It didn't matter what. I knew I couldn't describe, or understand, or explain my state of mind, but I felt able to function in front of the canvas and connect intuitively with my materials. I kept working. I don't recall if it was quiet, or if there were crowds of people still running at that time. I just

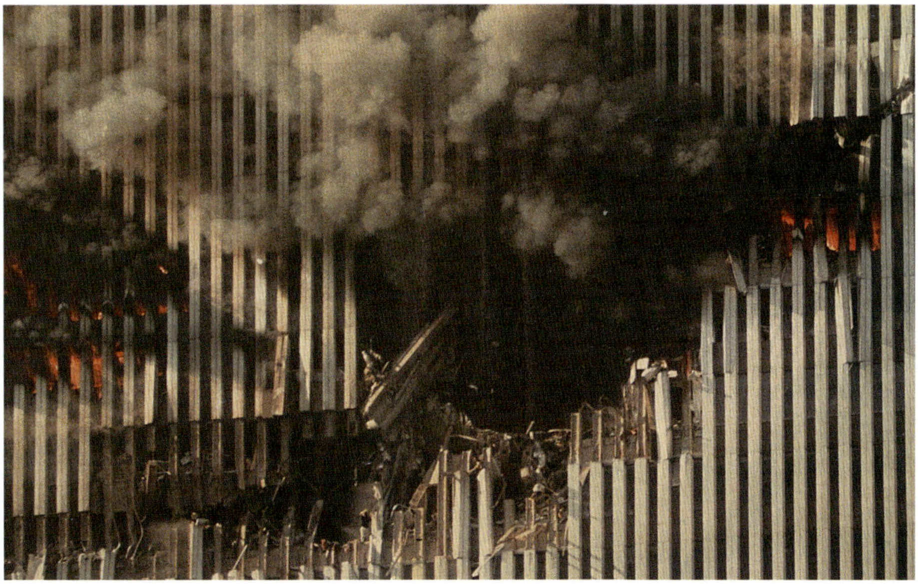

***Attack on the World Trade Center*, New York, 11 September 2001. Published in The New York Times,13 September 2001, p. A7. © The New York Times. Photograph: Brian Manning for The New York Times. Courtesy The New York Times.**

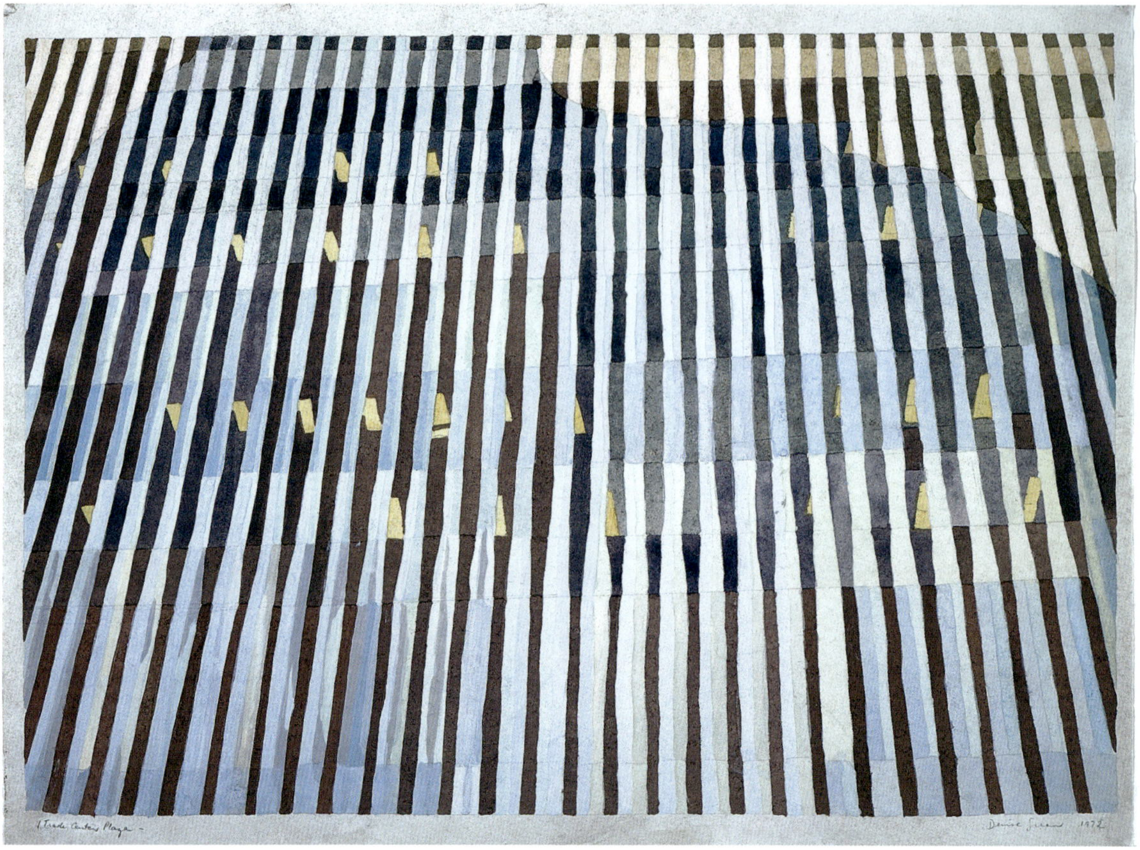

Denise Green, *World Trade Center Plaza*, 1972. Watercolour, 76 x 56 cm. Collection: Kerry Stokes, Perth, Australia. Photograph: Nicholas Walster.

sustained my concentration on the process of making the painting.

Around 5.00 pm I became concerned and walked down one block to the firehouse. The firemen were all safe. They told me that they had stayed together as a unit and were on the 28th floor when their chief heard some noise and decided to descend. They exited about one minute before the tower collapsed. Around 7.00 pm I walked to Madison and 30th Street and caught a bus to Frank's office. Families had been evacuated from Soho and they were on the bus with their suitcases.

Next morning I woke up thinking of a watercolour I had done in 1972 of the World Trade Center. It was a close-up view of the façade. I realized this image could function as a vertical pattern moving across the painting. In the studio I continued placing stripes across the canvas until I had oriented myself by making visual contact with the towers. They were south and west for me.

Not only did the tragedy cause a devastating loss of life, but it destroyed buildings that had many real and symbolic meanings. The towers gave a sense of orientation to many New Yorkers, they also functioned as a powerful hub of communication. Often people used to lift their eyes to the towers, symbols of power and wealth and modernity. Now, when they looked at the sky, there was only an absence.

The area around my building had been evacuated, but I kept to my usual schedule, arriving at the studio around 6.30 am each morning. I wanted to continue painting and developing the new image that had emerged, committed to making it part of my visual language.

I made other decisions during this period. The newspaper photos and televised images of the damaged towers made such a strong impression that they risked interfering with my memory of the attack. So I stopped looking at television and began reading European newspapers, like the *Manchester Guardian* and the *Herald Tribune*. I kept looking at the emptiness in the sky at the place where the World Trade Center had stood. The towers were gone, but in an odd way they still existed as insubstantial shadows.

During the first week after the attack, I made three large paintings, including the beginning of *Re-Witnessing*. Ordinarily one would expect the format of a painting of the twin towers of the World Trade Center to be a vertical rectangle, but I was drawn to develop it as a large horizontal. In that way I began expanding laterally the pattern of stripes that was suggestive of the subject. Intuitively, without realizing it, the image

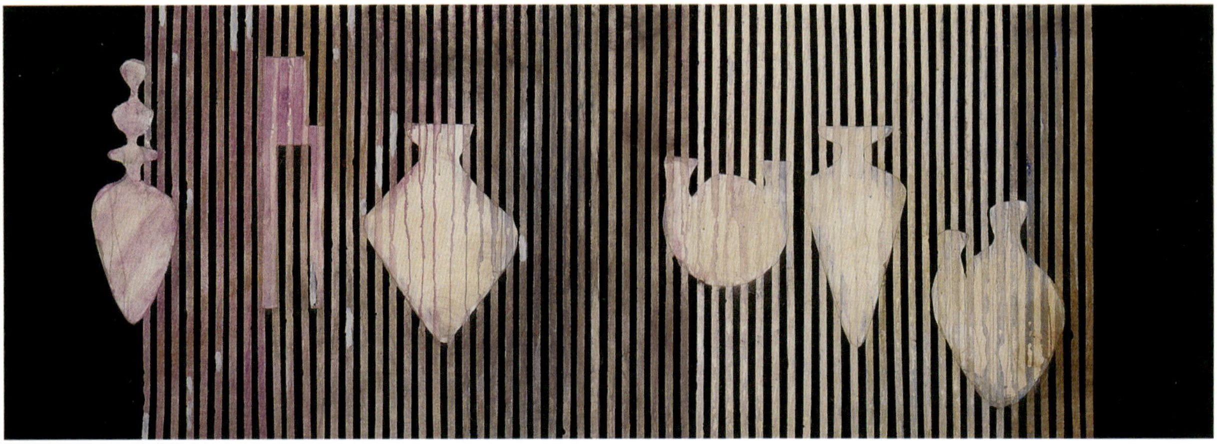

also depicted a picket fence that enclosed a space under the house of my childhood home. There, because it is situated in a tropical part of the country, the house is built on stilts, which raise it at about eight feet off the ground. There are slats of wood between the stilts and the effect is like a picket fence which encloses the area under the house while letting the sunlight in.

The picket fence and the area under the house brought memories back to me. It had been an area that had felt safe to me. The area under the house had become my creative and imaginative space. For years it had been a secret and private place for making drawings. But then some local youths invaded it. They were hostile and physically bullied me. I was terrified of them and recognised that because of their abuse it was dangerous to be there. It felt like a violation because they had entered what had been my safe space.

While people were emotionally shaken by the tragedy, the aftermath affected everyone differently in its reference to individual traumas from the past. My studio assistant, Carolina, was upset by the heightened police presence around my building. This reminded her of her home country, Argentina, and the disappearances and tortures that happened there. Perhaps I was so deeply shaken by the terrorist attacks because I had felt vulnerable to the youths' torment. I only realized later that the emotional power to the paintings that I did at that time had been fuelled by the earlier

Denise Green, *Re-Witnessing*, 2002. Acrylic on canvas, 112 x 315 cm. Collection: Kerry Stokes, Perth, Australia. Photograph: Nicholas Walster.

trauma that had occurred under the house. Thus, the same imagery of vertical stripes simultaneously points to three different meanings: present trauma, past trauma and creative space.

Two: Re-witnessing

Later changes in the painting resulted in my introducing shapes which referred to Etruscan vases, a very old theme in my work. I have written about the Etruscan vases and how they have a double meaning for me, functioning both as mundane or useful objects and as transcendent ones, connecting with an invisible realm. I wondered how the vase shapes connected to the vertical stripes and what their symbolic meaning is for me. Perhaps it is about the need to assert my aesthetic self in a painting associated with so much trauma?

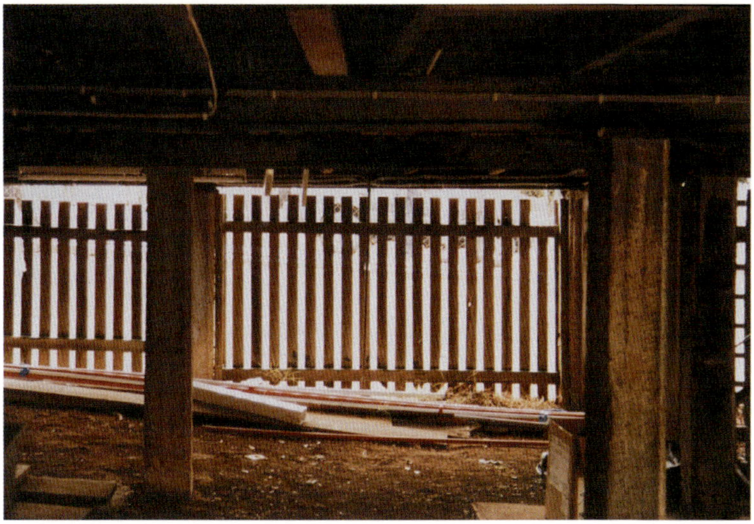

Denise Green, *Under the House*, 2003. Colour photograph.

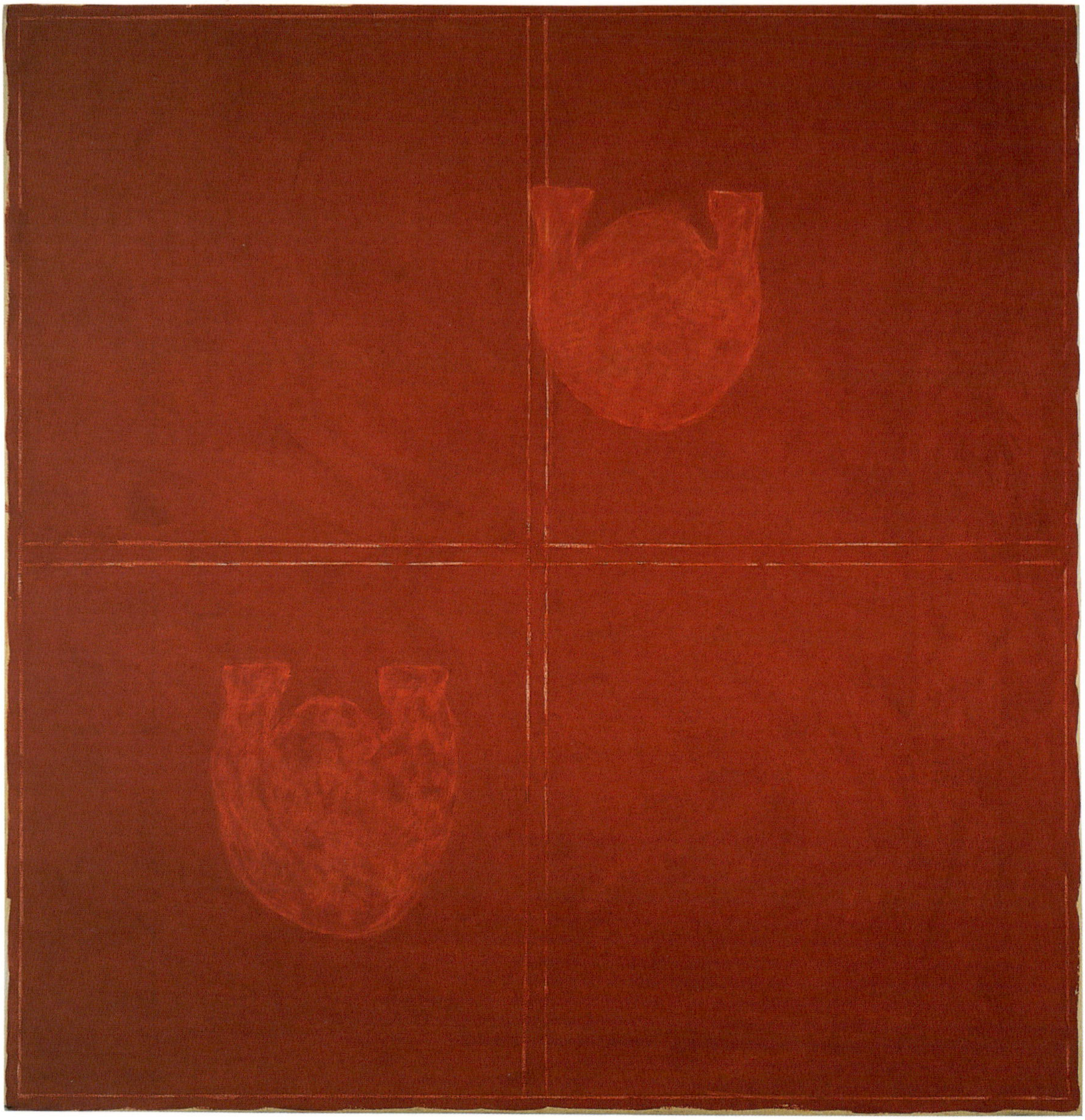

Denise Green, *Ghost Vases*, 1977. Oil on canvas, 160 x 160 cm. Collection: Angela and Nicholas Curtis, Sydney.

Bibliography

Benjamin, Walter. 'The Work of Art in the Age of Mechanical Reproduction', *Illuminations*, New York: Harcourt, Brace & World, 1968

Cree, Laura Murray. 'Resonating: Denise Green: A synergy of form and feeling', *Art & Australia*, Sydney, vol. 39, December 2001, pp. 224-226

Eliade, Marcel. *The Sacred and the Profane*, New York: Harcourt Brace, 1959

Fong Wen, C. *Beyond Representation: Chinese Painting and Calligraphy*. New York: The Metropolitan Museum of Art; New Haven and London: Yale University Press, 1992

Green, Denise.'Ross Bleckner interviewed by Denise Green', *Painterly Thought*, Exhibition catalogue, Berlin: Raab Gallerie, 1994

Green, Denise.'Lorand Hegyi Interview', in conjunction with a panel discussion, *Ethnic Minorities in the Artworld*, Vienna: Museum Moderner Kunst Stiftung Ludwig, 1996

Greenberg, Clement. 'Towards a Newer Laocoon', *Partisan Review 7*, no. 4 (July-August 1940), reprinted in Francis Frascina, ed., *Pollock and After: The Critical Debate*, New York: Harper and Row, 1985

Livingston, Morna. *Steps to Water. The Ancient Stepwells of India*, New York: Princeton Architectural Press, 2002

Neale, Margo. *Yiribana: An Introduction to the Aboriginal and Torres Strait Island Collection*, Sydney: The Art Gallery of New South Wales, 1994.

Pramar, V.S. *Haveli: Wooden Houses and Mansions of Gujarat*, Ahmedabad: Grantha in association with Mapin, 1989

Ramanujan, A.K.'Is there an Indian Way of Thinking? An Informal Essay', included in *India through Hindu Categories,* edited by McKim Marriott, Sage Publications, 1980

Roland, Alan. *In Search of Self in India and Japan: Towards a Cross-Cultural Psychology*, Princeton: Princeton University Press, 1988

Roland, Alan.'Imagery and Symbolic Expression in Dreams and Art', *International Journal of Psychoanalysis* 3, New York, 1972

Roland, Alan. 'Imagery and the Self in Artistic Creativity and Psychoanalytic Literary Criticism', *The Psychoanalytic Review*, vol 68, No. 3, 1981

Rosenthal, Mark. *Abstraction in the Twentieth Century: Total Risk, Freedom, Discipline,* New York: The Solomon R. Guggenheim Museum

Rothko, Mark. 'The Ides of Art: The Attitudes of 10 Artists on Their Art and Contemporaneousness', *The Tiger's Eye # 2*, December 1947

Rothko, Mark. [Letter] In Edward Alden Jewell, 'The Realm of Art: A New Platform and Other Matters: "Globalism" Pops into View', *New York Times*, 13 June, 1943, p. 9, (With Adolph Gottlieb and probably the collaboration of Barnett Newman.)

Sandler, Irving. *A Sweeper-Up After Artists: A Memoir*, Thames & Hudson, 2003

Sandler, Irving.'Agnes Martin Interviewed by Irving Sandler', *Art Monthly (UK)* 169, 1993, p. 13

Seymour, Anne. *Joseph Beuys: Drawings*, London: Victoria & Albert Museum, 1983

Singer, Milton. *When a great tradition modernizes: An anthropological approach to Indian civilization*, New York: Praeger, 1972

Sze, Mai-Mai. *The Way of Chinese Painting*, New York: Vintage Books, 1959

Tisdale, Caroline. *Joseph Beuys*, New York: The Solomon R. Guggenheim Museum, 1979

Varnedoe, Kirk. 'Inscriptions in Arcadia' in *Cy Twombly: A Retrospective*, New York: Museum of Modern Art, 1995

Index

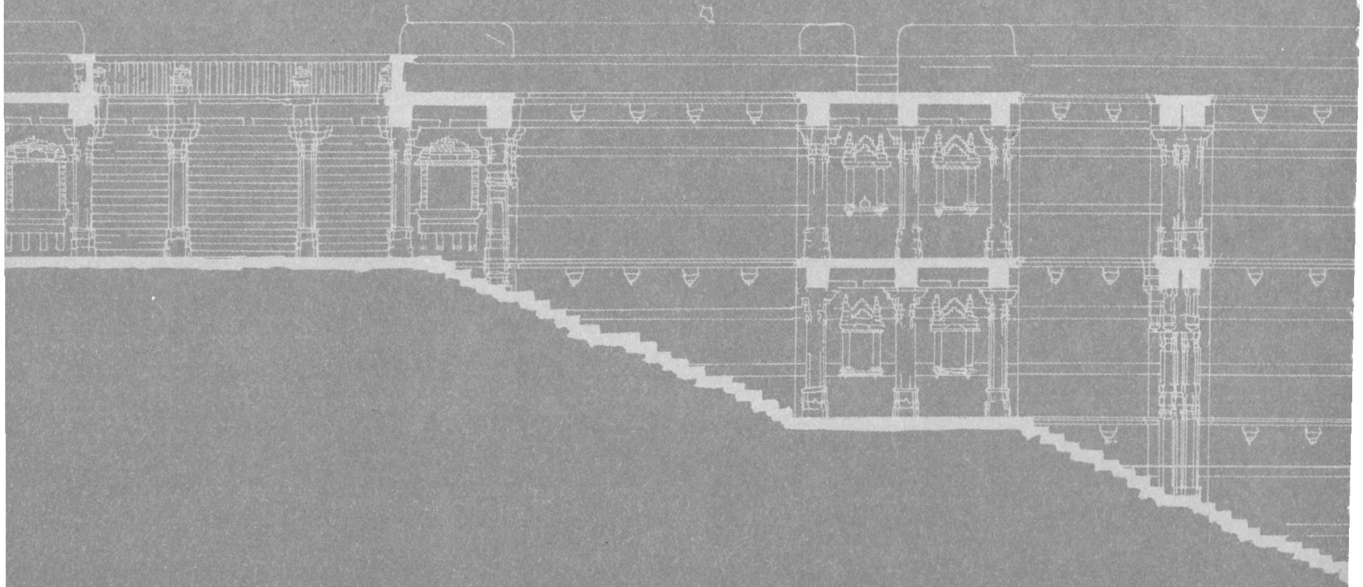